The Insider's Guide to Outsmart the SAT

NEW EDITION

SAT® 2-Second Shortcuts

Dr. Jay's Top 8 Shortcuts

SCORE FAST

0:02 0:00

PICK UP **200** EXTRA POINTS

THE BEST KEPT SECRETS IN SAT PREP ARE **INSIDE**

SEE THE SMART STRATEGY YOU ARE MISSING »»»»»

*SAT is a registered trademark of the College Entrance Examination Board which was not involved in the production of, and does not endorse, this product.

Carol Jay Stratoudakis, Ph.D.

Printed in the United States of America
17 16 15 14 13 12 11 10 9 8 7 6 5 4 3 2 1

ISBN 978-1-944068-45-5

To my parents

Acknowledgments

First and foremost, I would like to thank my husband Jim and my son Alex whose constant love and support made this book possible.

I am enormously grateful to my publisher, Deborah Herman, CEO, Micro Publishing Media, Inc., for her excellence.

Many thanks to Jane McWhorter and Rose Tannenbaum, my wonderful designers, who captured my vision and worked with me in great detail to make the book so user friendly.

Special thanks to family and friends for so much encouragement: Gary Colello and Patti Colello, Joyce Rechtschaffen and Lloyd Guerci, Marc and Kristen Lohser, Paige Panda, Julia Stratoudakis, Cynthia Turner, Rose Hayden, Al Domroe, Len Perlman, John Rotante, Jerry Rotante, Marian Fink, Sumbal Liaquat, Bobbie Olson, Kimberly MacDonald, Elaine Stephens, and Michelle Johnston.

Finally, thank you to all my students who inspired me to find a way to simplify the SAT.

Attention:
Parents, Tutors, and Coaches

Your students will *stress less* and *score more points* when they go to their SAT test with a set of SAT Shortcuts that give them a powerful new strategy to collect the **50-200 additional points** they need to reach their SAT Goal:

> ▶ *A high enough score* to be admitted to the college they would most like to attend.
> ▶ *A high enough score* to qualify for a scholarship.
> ▶ *A high enough score* to be recruited to play a college sport.

Table of Contents

Introduction

Success in life is about acting on opportunities. Success on the SAT is about acting on all the opportunities the Shortcuts give you to reach your highest possible SAT score.

The 8 Shortcuts plus the Bonus Shortcut put an end to the "old school" thinking that there are no quick and easy shortcuts to success on the SAT. This thinking is **completely false!** Each Shortcut opens your eyes to opportunities you have never seen before to quickly and easily increase your score—*without studying*. Only rapid scanning practice is required to learn how to recognize the Shortcuts.

It is time to **STOP** following the old advice to skip all the questions that look too hard to answer and **START** following Dr. Jay's Golden Rule to increase your SAT score faster than you ever thought possible.

> ## DR. JAY'S GOLDEN RULE
>
> **Before you start to use the process of elimination (POE), ALWAYS look for a pattern in an SAT question that will give you a Shortcut to the answer.**

SAT: 2 Second Shortcuts are the best kept secrets to success on the SAT test that you will not find in any other test prep book or course. You own it to yourself to now **SEE** all the **REAL SHORTCUTS TO SUCCESS** on the SAT you have been missing.

PART I
THE POWER OF THE SHORTCUTS

SHORTCUTS

Whoever You Are, the Shortcuts Work for You

No matter who you are, when you are taking the SAT, or what SAT scores you are aiming to achieve, the Shortcuts are for you. The Shortcuts give every student the fastest and easiest strategy to find more SAT answers and instantly increase their score.

You are a senior taking the SAT for the second time.

You took the SAT last spring, now you are taking it again this fall. On your last practice SAT test, your score remained the same, give or take a few points. You know if you keep preparing for the SAT in exactly the same way as you did before, you are likely to get the same results. You need to add another strategy to your skill set to bump your score up to a higher level. You would like to increase your score 50 points or more to reach the average SAT score for admission to the colleges and universities you would most like to attend. The Shortcuts give you exactly what you need: an extra strategy to take to your test to score more points.

You are a junior taking the SAT for the first time.

You are taking the SAT for the first time this spring. You went online and registered, then took a big gulp after committing to the test date. Now you are seriously starting to prep for the test. You know a few shortcuts to answer math questions, but you have never learned a Shortcut to help you answer reading and writing questions. In the reading section, you would definitely like to have a set of Shortcuts at your fingertips to correctly answer more of the 52 questions in this section. You know the more reading questions you can answer within the 65 minute time limit, the better your chance to reach your SAT goal.

You are a high school honor student aspiring to attend an Ivy League school.

You are challenging yourself to excel in AP or IB courses, earn the highest possible GPA, and get a high enough score to be considered for admission to the top colleges and universities in the U.S. You know you need to increase your SAT math score by 50 points to reach the average score earned by the students who were recently admitted to the Ivy League school you would most like to attend. Every time you take another SAT practice test, you keep getting the same math score. You realize if you keep approaching the math questions the same way, you are likely to keep getting the same results. You know you can definitely use an extra-scoring strategy to quickly add 50 points to your math score.

You are a high school athlete competing for a spot on a college team

Your coach informed you that you need to reach a certain reading or math SAT score to be considered for admission or to be eligible for an athletic scholarship. You know the value of speed in your sport, and you could use the speed the Shortcuts give you to cut through the answer choices and answer more questions when you are under the pressure of the time limits set for each section of the SAT.

You are a foreign student aspiring to earn an undergraduate degree from a college or university in the U.S.

You are from another country. Your first language is not English. You can add Shortcuts to your test-taking strategy to reduce the amount of English you have to read and think about in each SAT question. The Shortcuts offer you a huge competitive advantage over other foreign students taking the SAT.

You are a procrastinator

You normally cram for tests and actually do well when you study at the last minute. The Shortcut strategy that requires no studying is perfect for you. Only scanning practice is required to master a Shortcut. You can put the scanning skills you use to play video games to work snapping up Shortcuts. Select 3 Shortcuts in this book that look like they would be the most helpful to you. Set aside 20 minutes to learn each Shortcut. Within an hour, you will have 3 powerful Shortcuts at your finger tips to instantly help you reach the minimum score you need for college admission.

The Shortcut
BREAKOUT Strategy

All you have to do to increase your SAT score fast is ***BREAK OUT*** of the habit of exclusively relying on the process of elimination (POE) to answer all SAT questions and ***BREAK INTO*** the habit of first using Shortcuts. As soon as you start answering SAT questions by first taking 2 seconds to look for a Shortcut, you will experience the extra-scoring-power the Shortcuts give you when you are under the time pressure built into every section of the SAT. Time to:

 STOP thinking there are no quick and easy Shortcuts to success on the SAT.

 START believing there are many quick and easy Shortcuts to maximize your success on the SAT.

 STOP looking at 4 random answer choices to SAT questions.

 START recognizing distinct, little patterns in the 4 answer choices that give you a Shortcut to many SAT answers.

 STOP relying only on the longer process of elimination (POE) strategy to answer <u>all</u> SAT reading, writing, and math questions.

 START using the shorter pattern recognition strategy the Shortcuts give you to quickly answer <u>many</u> SAT reading, writing, and math questions.

STOP thinking that decisions on the SAT made slowly and deliberately by reading and thinking about all the information put into a question are better than decisions made very quickly based on less information.

 START thinking that decisions on the SAT made very quickly by reading and thinking about less information are just as good as decisions made slowly and deliberately based on all the available information.

 STOP thinking: "slow and steady wins the race."

 START thinking: On the SAT I can "cut to the chase" by taking Shortcuts to the answers.

The Shortcut TOP SECRET PATTERNS

All the Shortcuts in this book are based on the belief that decisions made very quickly by using a bit of information provided by a simple pattern in an SAT question are just as good as decisions made more slowly by using the traditional process of elimination (POE). While in many situations in life, the best strategy is slow and steady wins the race, the simple patterns embedded in the SAT change this reality. Now there is a strategy to win the race and reach your goal on the SAT that values speed.

The patterns in SAT questions speed up the process of answering SAT questions. The instant you detect a secret pattern, this inside information gives you a Shortcut to the correct answer. Some patterns in the answer choices instantly identify the 2 best answer choices for you and give you a 50% chance to score a point without thinking about the choices. Other patterns instantly identify 3 answer choices and give you a 33% chance to score a point without thinking about the choices. One pattern identifies the 1 best answer choice that gives you a near 100% chance to score a point.

The Shortcut
HUGE SCORING ADVANTAGES

The split-second you recognize a simple pattern in an SAT reading, writing, or math question, you get 5 huge scoring advantages no other SAT strategy offers. The advantages are:

 INSTANT SCORING ADVANTAGE #1: Eliminates Answer Choices
The Shortcuts eliminate wrong answer choices for you. As a result, you do not have to read or think about all the confusing and irrelevant information loaded into all the wrong answer choices that distract you from identifying the correct answer.

 INSTANT SCORING ADVANTAGE#2: Turns Hard Questions into Easier Questions
By eliminating answer choices for you, the Shortcuts immediately reduce the difficulty of SAT questions. For example, Math Shortcut #8 cuts the difficulty of a math question in half (50%) by reducing the answer choices from 4 possibilities to the 2 most likely answers.

 INSTANT SCORING ADVANTAGE#3: Saves Time, Effort, and Mental Energy
Every time you use a Shortcut, you save all the time it normally take you to complete the process of elimination (POE) – anywhere from 30 seconds to 1 minute per question. This is an enormous time savings when you are under the time limits set for every section of the SAT.

 INSTANT SCORING ADVANTAGE #4: Turns Questions Previously Omitted into New Scoring Opportunities
The Shortcuts give you a simple strategy to answer:
▶ questions you previously had no clue where to begin to answer,
▶ questions you previously skipped because they looked too intimidating to try to answer,
▶ questions you previously never had time to go back to answer.

 INSTANT SCORING ADVANTAGE #5: Reduces Stress Before the Test
After seeing plenty of Shortcuts in your SAT practice tests, you stress less because you know you can count on the Shortcuts to help you answer more questions and collect more points. Instead of stressing before the test, you are psyched to achieve the same success on your actual SAT as you achieved on your practice SAT tests by using Shortcuts.

YOUR MASTER GAME PLAN

Your game plan is to take advantage of all the Shortcuts hidden-in-plain-sight to reach your SAT goal. Your new approach to answering SAT questions is to FIRST look for a Shortcut. For all the SAT questions that do not contain a Shortcut, you are prepared to use the more deliberate process of elimination (POE). Your winning combination of strategies is: **Shortcuts** + **POE** to get the results you want as fast as possible.

Set a Realistic Goal

It is important to set a realistic goal. How much you can increase your score depends upon your starting point and how much effort you put into learning the Shortcuts. For starters, aim to reach a score that is 50 points higher than the score you received on your PSAT or a recent SAT. *Fifty points is often the all-important gap closer between the score you currently have and the score you need to reach.* Adding 50 points to your score may be enough to increase your chances for college admission, for a scholarship, or for eligibility to play a college sport.

As soon as you learn a few Shortcuts, you will be surprised how fast you can add 50 points to your SAT score. The following chart shows you how the points add up.

HOW 50 POINTS ADDS UP FAST

USE　　**Shortcuts #1, #5, or #8 to answer 10 questions**

GET　　**5 correct answers**
By the law of chance (like flipping a coin), you are likely to get 5 out of the 10 questions correct (50%).

COLLECT　　**50 points**
Each correct answer adds roughly 10 points to your score
5 correct answers x 10 points per answer = 50 points

How to Get the Results You Want

You can get the results you want on your next practice SAT test. All you have to do is:

▶ **1**. Memorize the 8 secret patterns revealed to you in this book that give you simple, little Shortcuts to SAT answers.

▶ **2** Develop your ability to recognize a Shortcut in a split-second by completing the Practice Drills provided for each Shortcut.

▶ **3**. Pick out a practice test in any SAT workbook. Scan this test for examples of Shortcuts. The more examples of Shortcuts you find, the more psyched you will be to use Shortcuts to get the SAT results you want.

▶ **4**. Go ahead and take another practice test. Challenge yourself to snap up 20 Shortcuts to get the results you want.

▶ **5**. See how many points you added to your SAT or PSAT scores by using 20 Shortcuts! Keep using your favorite Shortcuts on every practice test you take to reach your highest possible SAT scores.

▶ **6**. Plan to achieve the same great results on your real SAT test as you achieved on your practice SAT tests.

PART II
TOP SECRET SHORTCUTS

RULE

<u>**WHEN 2 answer choices to an SAT reading question contain the same word(s), THEN 1 of these 2 choices is the correct answer.**</u> The same word(s) may appear at the beginning of 2 answer choices, at the end of 2 answer choices, or in different locations.

SECRET PATTERN
2 answer choices contain the same word(s):

(A) xxxxxxxxxxxxxxxxxxxx
(B) **carriage** xxxxxxxxxxxxxxxx
(C) xxxxxxxxxxxxxxxx
(D) **carriage** xxxxxxxxxxxxx

REWARD

The second you RECOGNIZE this secret pattern you get the POWER to ELIMINATE 2 answer choices and PREDICT (B) or (D) is the correct answer.

Reading Shortcut #1: EXAMPLES

The following 3 examples of Reading Shortcut #1 are SNAPSHOTS that show you how easy it is to recognize the secret Shortcut #1 is based on: **the same words in 2 answer choices.** The first example presents **the same word(s) at the beginning of 2 answer choices.** The second example presents **the same word(s) at the end of 2 answer choices.** The third example presents **the same word(s) in different locations.**

EXAMPLE #1: BEFORE

Before you recognize the Shortcut, the SAT question is **difficult**. It is longer and harder to answer with 4 possible answers to read and think about.

1. The reference to breakfast cereal bars (lines 16-21) supports the position that
   (A) claims of nutritional value are questionable
   (B) cereal bars are no substitute for a hot breakfast
   (C) limited research is used to make broad statements
   (D) claims of health benefits inflate product price

❖ ❖ ❖ EXAMPLE #1: AFTER ❖ ❖ ❖

After you recognize the Shortcut, the question is **simplified**. It is shorter and easier to answer with only 2 possible answers to read and think about.

1. The reference to breakfast cereal bars (lines 16-21) supports the position that
   (A) **claims of** nutritional value are questionable
   (D) **claims of** health benefits inflate product price

Before you start to use the process of elimination (POE) to answer an SAT reading question, take *2 seconds* to scan the answer choices for this **secret pattern**: *2 answer choices that <u>begin</u> with the same word(s).*

DETECT

"claims of" <u>at the beginning</u> of answer choices (A) and (D).

PREDICT

(A) or (D) is the correct answer.
Rule out the other choices!

DECIDE

either (A) or (D).
When you are totally clueless, just pick (A) or (D).
By the law of chance, you **get a great 50% chance** to select the correct answer.
When you have a clue to tip your decision in favor of (A) or (D), go for it.
By using a bit of knowledge you **get a much higher than 50% chance** to select the correct answer.

SCORE

1 correct answer	*gives you*	**1 (raw) point**
1 (raw) point	*roughly adds*	**10 points to your SAT score**

EXAMPLE #2: BEFORE

Before you recognize the Shortcut, the SAT question is **difficult**. It is longer and harder to answer with 4 possible answers to read and think about.

2. It can be inferred from the passage that the author's parents were
    (A) disappointed in his behavior in school
    (B) out of touch with the demands of extra-curricular activities
    (C) unaware of how much bullying goes on in school
    (D) unavailable to help him manage homework

❖ ❖ ❖ EXAMPLE #2: AFTER ❖ ❖ ❖

After you recognize the Shortcut, the question is **simplified**. It is shorter and easier to answer with only 2 possible answers to read and think about.

2. It can be inferred from the passage that the author's parents were
    (A) disappointed by the author's poor grades **in school**
    (C) unaware of how much bullying goes on **in school**

Before you start to use the process of elimination (POE) to answer an SAT reading question, take **2 seconds** to scan the answer choices for this **secret pattern**: *2 answer choices that <u>end</u> with the same word(s).*

DETECT

"**in school**" <u>at the end</u> of answer choices (A) and (C).

PREDICT

(A) or (C) is the correct answer.
Rule out the other answer choices!

DECIDE

either (A) or (C).
When you are totally clueless, just pick (A) or (C).
By the law of chance, you **get a great 50% chance** to select the correct answer.
When you have a clue to tip your decision is favor of (A) or (C), go for it.
By using a bit of knowledge, you **get a much higher than 50% chance** to select the correct answer.

SCORE

| 1 correct answer | *gives you* | 1 (raw) point |
| 1 (raw) point | *roughly adds* | 10 points to your SAT score |

EXAMPLE #3: BEFORE

Before you recognize the Shortcut, the SAT question is **difficult**. It is longer and harder to answer with 4 possible answers to read and think about.

3. The exchange between the narrator and the airport security officer (lines 25-47) is best described as
   (A) an argument over the personality characteristics of leaders
   (B) a debate about the fairness of the criteria used in developing ethnic labels
   (C) a discussion of the rules of survival in a gang culture
   (D) an attempt to defend the use of ethnic labels in law enforcement

❖ ❖ ❖ EXAMPLE #3: AFTER ❖ ❖ ❖

After you recognize the Shortcut, the question is **simplified**. It is shorter and easier to answer with only 2 possible answers to read and think about.

3. The exchange between the narrator and the airport security officer (lines 25-47) is best described as
   (B) A debate over the fairness of criteria used in developing **ethnic labels**
   (D) An attempt to defend the use of **ethnic labels** in law enforcement

Before you start to use the process of elimination (POE) to answer an SAT reading question, take *2 seconds* to scan the answer choices for this **secret pattern**: *2 answer choices that have the same word(s) in __different locations__*.

DETECT

"ethnic labels" __in different locations__ in answer choices (B) and (D).

PREDICT

(B) or (D) is the correct answer.
Rule out the other answer choices!

DECIDE

either (B) or (D).
When you are totally clueless, just pick (B) or (D).
By the law of chance, you **get a great 50% chance** to select the correct answer.

When you have a clue to tip your decision in favor of (B) or (D), go for it.
By using a bit of knowledge, you **get a much higher than 50% chance** to select the correct answer.

SCORE

| 1 correct answer | *gives you* | 1 (raw) point |
| 1 (raw) point | *roughly adds* | 10 points to your SAT score! |

The POWER of KNOWING How to Analyze Answer Choices

After seeing Reading Shortcut #1, you have the power of knowing exactly which secret pattern to look for in the answer choices that will give you an instant Shortcut to identify the 2 best answer choices you never recognized before.

Reading Shortcut #1: Speed Practice Drills

Now it is time to practice using Reading Shortcut #1 to access opportunities to score on your SAT in a ***split-second*** – *as fast as you click on Google or tap an app on your smartphone.* The questions in the drills are designed to develop your ability to rapidly scan the answer choices to detect this Shortcut: ***2 answer choices contain the same word(s).*** *The same words may appear at the beginning or end of 2 answer choices or in different locations.*

The repetition built into the 3 drills will make scanning the answer choices for Reading Shortcut #1 a part of your test-taking routine – a new habit to locate the best answers choices faster than ever before possible. The faster you can snap up Shortcut #1 in the following drills, the better prepared you will be to take advantage of this Shortcut to answer more questions and score more points on your SAT.

Shortcut #1
Speed Practice Drill A

1. The description of a typical high school athlete in lines 59-64 underscores the narrator's concern about the

(A) emphasis placed on speed in sports
(B) intense pressure on athletes to excel
(C) emphasis on winning at all costs
(D) increase in the use of steroids

2. In lines 24-27, the narrator acknowledges which of the following points:

(A) scientific results require verification over time
(B) observations should be substantiated by facts
(C) research studies have unintended consequences
(D) scientific theories evolve through trial and error

3. The author suggests that the "silence" of the school board indicated

(A) opposition to the parent's proposal
(B) an unwillingness to accept any new proposal
(C) a reluctance to continue the discussion
(D) disagreement with the request to fund a pilot study

4. The narrator's critique (lines 32-43) supports the position that

(A) cosmetic procedures can be more harmful than beneficial
(B) medical practice should cure illness, not improve beauty
(C) insurance companies cannot legally cover cosmetic procedures
(D) advertising surgery as "quick and easy" is misleading

5. The author references technology in the third paragraph most likely to

(A) suggest a vision for twenty-first century learning

(B) observe the impact of cell phones in the classroom

(C) argue that the internet will continue to change education

(D) suggest an advancement in computer-based instruction

6. The author references chemical companies (lines 49-55) in order to

(A) call attention to manufacturers of harmful chemicals

(B) provide examples of corporate compliance with regulations

(C) raise concern about the disposal of industrial waste

(D) point out excellent examples of environmental protection

7. The author of Passage 1 would most likely regard the phenomena described in lines 6-12 as

(A) an observation worthy of serious investigation

(B) an event that adds to the mystery of The Last Supper

(C) an incident that raises concerns among art collectors

(D) a coincidence that enhances the value of The Last Supper

8. In lines 33-46 the narrator encourages readers to view sleep deprivation as

(A) a cause of attention deficit disorder (ADD) in older children

(B) an issue that requires lifestyle adjustments

(C) a reminder of a basic human need

(D) a factor that contributes to obesity in children

9. The author would most likely agree with which of the following statements

(A) children require close supervision around swimming pools

(B) swimming pools are dangerous for all age groups

(C) safety concerns outweigh creative play opportunities

(D) resale advantages out number the disadvantages of swimming pools

10. In line 25, the term "fading" refers to the fact that the narrator

(A) felt himself slipping into depression

(B) had health issues that depleted his energy

(C) realized he needed to reach out to friends

(D) thought friends were tired of waiting for him

Check the Answer Key on the next page.

ANSWER KEY

Reading Shortcut #1: Speed Practice Drill A

Same Word(s)	Best Choices	Answer
1. emphasize	1. A or C	1. A
2. scientific	2. A or D	2. D
3. proposal	3. A or B	3. B
4. cosmetic procedures	4. A or C	4. C
5. suggest	5. A or D	5. A
6. examples	6. B or D	6. B
7. The Last Supper	7. B or D	7. D
8. children	8. A or D	8. D
9. swimming pools	9. A, B, or D*	9. A
10. friends	10. C or D	10. C

Note: In some SAT reading questions, you will find the same word(s) in 3 answer choices.

SCORE BOX

Total Number of Correct Answers	Total Points Added to Your Score
1	10
2	20
3	30
4	40
5	50
6	60
7	70
8	80
9	90
10	100

Reminder: 1 correct answer adds roughly 10 points to your SAT score.

Shortcut #1
Speed Practice Drill B

DIRECTIONS:
▶ Set your timer or timer app for 60 seconds.
▶ Underline the same word(s) in 2 answer choices.
▶ Circle 1 choice – without thinking about the 2 choices.

Experience the power you get to identify the 2 best answer choices in a split-second!

1. The author's assumption in the fourth paragraph (lines 56-70) is that
(A) the interpretation of a painting is driven by experience
(B) responses to any art form are unpredictable
(C) light triggers a range of emotional reactions
(D) responses from men and women vary in intensity

2. The author of Passage 1 and the author of Passage 2 are similar in that both
(A) argue the construction of a typical city park has no lasting benefit
(B) agree random developments have a negative impact on the aesthetic appeal of a neighborhood
(C) think random developments have attracted single, professional people
(D) feel landlords need to invest in landscaping their residential property

3. The primary purpose of the last paragraph (lines 43-69) is to
(A) question the new modes for acquiring information
(B) suggest that some compromise is possible between old and new modes of acquiring information
(C) long for an earlier form of research that relied on extensive reading of printed books
(D) outline the differences between search engines to access data online

4. In context, the word "connectivity" (line 11) describes the
(A) moment when a message is received
(B) mode of thinking that characterizes communication today
(C) process through which people share information
(D) contrast between effective and ineffective methods of communication

5. The author of Passage 2 would most likely argue that the survey (Passage 1, lines 11-18) is

(A) less representative of diversity
(B) more representative of diversity
(C) inclusive of all ethnic groups
(D) designed to replicate previous studies

6. In context, the reference to the "evolving plot" (line 16) serves to emphasize

(A) historical interest in murder mysteries
(B) underlying similarities between past events
(C) challenges in uncovering historical mysteries
(D) author's talent for creating fictional criminals

7. The author mentions George Bush (line 9) primarily in order to

(A) cite one president who represents a certain American perspective
(B) describe the reward of one president's determination
(C) illustrate that global leaders attempt to contribute to world peace
(D) stress the fast that the Middle East does not embrace Western values

8. The primary purpose of the passage is to

(A) expose the private agenda of a man chairing a business meeting
(B) chronicle the peculiar behavior of a travelling businessman
(C) provide a detailed description of a day in the life of a travelling businessman
(D) explain the underlying motives for tape recording a speech

9. The author refers to John's "stripe tie" (line 34) in order to suggest

(A) the importance John places on his professional appearance
(B) his ability to command respect from his audience by wearing a tie
(C) his belief that wearing a tie elevates the importance of his comments
(D) his awareness that senior executives value formal attire at work

10. According to the author of Passage 2, which of the following is true about the statement in lines 19-20?

(A) It was not a commonly held belief among the troops.
(B) Only the most pessimistic followers were unconvinced
(C) It would be disproved if the General was successful.
(D) It was a belief held by the First Families of Virginia.

Check the Answer Key on the next page.

ANSWER KEY

Reading Shortcut#1: Speed Practice Drill B

Same Word(s)	Best Choices	Answer
1. responses	1. B or D	1. B
2. random developments have	2. B or C	2. C
3. new modes, acquiring information	3. A or B	3. A
4. communication	4. B or D	4. D
5. representative of diversity	5. A or B	5. A
6. historical, mysteries	6. A or C	6. C
7. one, president or president's *	7. A or B	7. B
8. travelling businessman	8. B or C	8. C
9. wearing a tie	9. B or C	9. B
10. It was, belief	10. A or D	10. D

*Note: The possessive form of a word is treated as the "same word."

SCORE BOX

Total Number of Correct Answers	Total Points Added to Your Score
1	10
2	20
3	30
4	40
5	50
6	60
7	70
8	80
9	90
10	100

Reminder: 1 correct answer adds roughly 10 points to your SAT score.

Shortcut #1
Speed Practice Drill C

1. The last 2 sentences of Passage 1 (lines 72-80) suggests that the narrator

(A) recognizes that conflicts are often rooted in ethnic differences

(B) believes in the equal distribution of natural resources

(C) thinks political unrest emerges from religious intolerance

(D) believes that economic inequality causes civil disputes

2. Passage 2 most strongly suggests that which of the following is true of Mr. Green?

(A) He acts on his belief in the mind and body connection.

(B) He is afraid to try new approaches to reducing stress.

(C) He likes to try new approaches to meditation.

(D) He questions the value of religious rituals.

3. Which claim from the passage is supported by the graphic?

(A) A person's focus can be improved through mindfulness techniques.

(B) Any person can benefit from learning how to practice mindfulness.

(C) Breathing exercises help children learn to "calm down."

(D) Counselors view meditation as a form of relaxation therapy.

4. It can be reasonably inferred that which of the following is true?

(A) None of the men were skilled divers.

(B) Some of the men were skilled divers.

(C) The narrator is the only man with diving experience.

(D) The divers are unwilling to return home empty handed.

5. The author of Passage 2 most likely chose to write about the space ship to
(A) raise questions about prevailing beliefs
(B) provide insights into the history of space flight
(C) commemorate a unique example of flight in space
(D) call attention to the future of space exploration

6. Based on the passage, why do the narrator's parents change their minds about letting him go on the field trip?
(A) They decide they could trust the adult organizing the trip.
(B) They want to encourage the narrator to develop new friendships.
(C) They decide there is adequate supervision for the size of the group.
(D) They know several of the participating students.

7. It can be reasonably inferred that the judge would support which of the following recommendations:
(A) increase in summer job training programs
(B) development of job training programs for juvenile offenders
(C) expansion of vocational education in high school
(D) creation of apprenticeships in fast growing industries

8. According to the first two paragraphs, what claim does the author seek to refute?
(A) The belief that the dictionary is the best authority to resolve board game disputes.
(B) The assumption that students still rely on dictionaries to spell check their work.
(C) The notion that the dictionary is an absolute authority in schools.
(D) The prediction that dictionaries will become obsolete over time.

9. The passage most strongly suggests that which of the following statements is true?
(A) The guest speaker was warmly welcomed when he arrived at the conference.
(B) The guest speaker received criticism for his decision to attend the conference.
(C) The authorities feared protestors would interrupt the proceedings.
(D) The audience was prepared to evacuate the auditorium in an orderly fashion.

10. The main rhetorical effect of the final paragraph (lines 82-95) is to
(A) emphasize Patrick's deep sense of commitment to his job
(B) foreshadow the conflict between Patrick and his co-workers
(C) illustrate the strength of Patrick's work ethic
(D) provide a resolution to the conflict Patrick faced

ANSWER KEY

Reading Shortcut #1: Speed Practice Drill C

Same Word(s)	Best Choices	Answer
1. believes	1. B or D	1. D
2. try new approaches	2. B or C	2. B
3. person, mindfulness	3. A or B	3. A
4. of the men were skilled divers	4. A or B	4. B
5. space, flight	5. B or C	5. C
6. They decide	6. A or C	6. C
7. job training programs	7. A or B	7. B
8. dictionary, authority	8. A or C	8. A
9. guest speaker, conference	9. A or B	9. A
10. Patrick, conflict	10. B or D	10. D

SCORE BOX

Total Number of Correct Answers	Total Points Added to Your Score
1	10
2	20
3	30
4	40
5	50
6	60
7	70
8	80
9	90
10	100

Reminder: 1 correct answer adds roughly 10 points to your SAT score.

Practice in Your SAT Workbooks

After completing the 3 Speed Practice Drills, you are the *all-seeing, all-knowing,* newly-minted **MASTER** of Reading Shortcut #1. Now you can put it to work for you.

Go to the Official SAT Study Guide published by The College Board which contains <u>real</u> SAT practice tests. Scan the reading section to see more examples of Shortcut #1. *Seeing is believing!* The more examples you see, the more this Shortcut will *stick* in your mind and give you the extra-scoring power you need to reach the score you want on your SAT test.

> Nike tells you: *Just do it!*
>
> Dr. Jay tells you: *Just use it!*
>
> *Just use it* on every practice test you take, and you will be ready to snap up all the examples of Shortcut #1 hidden inside your SAT test.

No Shortcut is Foolproof

Just as there are exceptions to every rule, there are exceptions to **Reading Shortcut #1.**

READING SHORTCUT #2

RULE

<u>**WHEN**</u> an SAT reading question asks for the "best evidence," THEN the 2 best answers are the 2 choices that are closest to the line number(s) in a prior question. *If the last line number(s) stated in a prior question is "line 19," then the 2 answer choices closest to "line 19" contain the correct answer.*

SECRET PATTERN

The 2 best answers are the 2 choices closest to the line number(s) stated in a prior question.

Prior Question with a Line Number:

As used in **line 19,** "clash" most nearly means
(A) xxxx
(B) xxxxxxxx
(C) xxxxx
(D) xxxxxxxx

"Best Evidence" Question:

Which choice provides the best evidence…
(A) Lines 18-20
(B) Lines 39-43
(C) Lines 48-51
(D) Lines 52-55

Lines 18-20 and Lines 39-43 are closest to "line 19."

Correct Answer: (A) or (B)

REWARD

The second you RECOGNIZE this pattern you get the POWER to PREDICT (A) or (B) is the correct answer.

Reading Shortcut #2: EXAMPLES

The following 2 examples of Shortcut #2 are SNAPSHOTS that show you how easy it is to recognize the **secret pattern** Shortcut #2 is based on: <u>**The 2 best answers are the 2 choices closest to the line number(s) stated in a prior question.**</u>

EXAMPLE #1: BEFORE

Before you recognize the Shortcut, the SAT question is **difficult**. It is longer and harder to answer with 4 possible answers to read and think about.

1. Which choice provides the best evidence…?
   (A) Lines 17-21 ("I thought…disappoint")
   (B) Lines 21-24 ("The demands…it")
   (C) Lines 44-47 ("Unaware…life")
   (D) Lines 68-74 ("The peer…manage")

❖ ❖ ❖ EXAMPLE #1: AFTER ❖ ❖ ❖

After you recognize the Shortcut, the question is **simplified**. It is shorter and easier to answer with only 2 answer choices to read and think about.

The Prior Question with Line Numbers:
In **lines 50-63** the author's reference to pets serves to

1. Which choice provides the best evidence…?
   (C) Lines 44-47 ("Unaware…life")
   (D) Lines 68-74 ("The peer…manage")

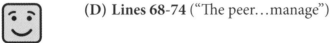

Before you start to use the process of elimination (POE) to answer an SAT reading question, take **2 seconds** to scan the prior questions for this **secret pattern:** *line number(s) stated in a prior question.*

DETECT

lines 50-63 in a prior question.

PREDICT

the 2 best answers are the 2 choices closest to lines 50-63.
Rule out the other choices!

DECIDE

either (C) Lines 44-47 or (D) Lines 68-74 is the correct answer.

When you are totally clueless, just pick (C) or (D). By law of chance, you **get a great 50% chance** to select the correct answer.

When you have a clue from the passage to tip your decision in favor of (C) or (D), go for it. By using a bit of knowledge, you **get a much higher than 50% chance** to select the correct answer.

SCORE

1 correct answer	gives you	1 (raw) point
1 (raw) point	roughly adds	10 points to your SAT score!

EXAMPLE #2: BEFORE

Before you recognize the Shortcut, the SAT question is **difficult**. It is longer and harder to answer with 4 possible answers to read and think about.

2. Which choice provides the best evidence…?
   (A) Lines 25-27 ("The age…change")
   (B) Lines 43-46 ("And now…life")
   (C) Lines 54-58 ("We need…force")
   (D) Lines 61-64 ("Day…opportunity")

❖ ❖ ❖ EXAMPLE #2: AFTER ❖ ❖ ❖

After you recognize the Shortcut, the question is **simplified.** It is shorter and easier to answer with only 2 answer choices to read and think about.

Prior Question with line number(s):
The author most likely uses the examples in **lines 23-28** to highlight

2. Which choice provides the best evidence…?

   (A) **Lines 25-27** ("The age…change")
   (B) **Lines 43-46** ("And now…life")

Before you start to use the process of elimination (POE) to answer an SAT reading question, take *2 seconds* to scan your prior questions for this **secret pattern:** *line number(s) stated in a prior question.*

DETECT

lines 23-28 in a prior question.

PREDICT

the 2 best answers are the 2 choices closest to lines 23-28.
Rule out the other answer choices!

DECIDE

either (A) Lines 25-27 or (B) Lines 43-46 is the correct answer.

When you are totally clueless, just pick (A) or (B). By the law of chance, you **get a great 50% chance** to select the correct answer.

When you have a clue from the passage to tip your decision in favor of (A) or (B), go for it. By using a bit of knowledge, you **get a much higher than 50% chance** to select the correct answer.

SCORE

| 1 correct answer | *gives you* | 1 (raw) point |
| 1 (raw) point | *roughly adds* | 10 points to your SAT score! |

The POWER of KNOWING How to Analyze Answer Choices

After seeing the Reading Shortcut #2, you have the power of knowing exactly which secret pattern to look for in your preceding questions that will give you an instant Shortcut to identify the correct answer you never recognized before.

Reading Shortcut #2: Speed Practice Drills

Now it is time to practice using Reading Shortcut #2 to access opportunities to score on your SAT in *a split-second – as fast as you click on Google or tap an app on your smartphone.* The questions in the drills are designed to develop your ability to detect this Shortcut: *the 2 best answers are the 2 choices that are closest to the line number(s) stated in a prior question.*

The repetition built into the 3 drills will make scanning the answer choices for Reading Shortcut #2 a part of your test-taking routine — a new habit to locate the best answer choices faster than ever before possible. The faster you can snap up Shortcut #2 in the following drills, the better prepared you will be to take advantage of this Shortcut to answer more questions and score more points on your SAT.

Shortcut #2
Speed Practice Drill A

DIRECTIONS:
▶ Set your timer or timer app for 60 seconds.
▶ Underline the line number(s) stated in the prior question.
▶ Underline the 2 answer choices that are closest to the line numbers in the prior question.
▶ Circle 1 answer.

EXAMPLE
Prior Question: The central idea of lines **69-80** is to

Which 2 choices provide the best evidence…?
(A) Line 43 ("Media. . .life")
(B) Lines 49-56 ("Yet. . . motherland")
(C) **Lines 65-75** ("Society. . . home")
(D) **Lines 81-82** ("They. . . mediate")
Correct Answer: (C) or (D)

Experience the power you get to locate the 2 best answer choices in 2 seconds!

Prior question: In line 21 the author of Passage 1 describes the state of the economy as a matter of urgency in order to
1. Which choice provides the best evidence…?
(A) Lines 19-23 ("It was…economy")
(B) Lines 25-30 ("They…material")
(C) Lines 30-31 ("This…resource")
(D) Lines 42-45 ("Claim…space")

Prior question: The author of Passage 2 identifies "the natives" (lines 19-22) to
2. Which choice provides the best evidence…?
(A) Lines 4-7 ("When…America")
(B) Lines 8-11 ("Their jobs…Somalia")
(C) Lines 20-26 ("The natives…city")
(D) Lines 27-29 ("Life…simpler")

Prior question: Why is the rebellion "fatal" (line 7-14)?

3. Which choice provides the best evidence…?

(A) Lines 9-12 ("The lack…classics")
(B) Lines 32-33 ("In a range…libraries")
(C) Lines 41-42 ("Critics…fiction")
(D) Lines 50-53 ("Since…they")

Prior question: The purpose of the information in lines 65-72 is to

4. Which choice provides the best evidence…?

(A) Line 43 ("Media…life")
(B) Lines 49-56 ("Yet…motherland")
(C) Lines 64-74 ("Society…home")
(D) Lines 81-82 ("They…meditate")

Prior question: The central idea of the second paragraph (lines 22-29) is that

5. Which choice provides the best evidence…?

(A) Line 29 ("If…author")
(B) Lines 32-34 ("The exception…held")
(C) Lines 48-49 ("Some…theory")
(D) Lines 62-63 ("The explanation…it")

Prior question: As used in line 35, "block" most nearly means

6. Which choice provides the best evidence…?

(A) Lines 3-7 ("Although…block")
(B) Lines 15-18 ("As the…remedies")
(C) Lines 19-25 ("Whereas…writer's")
(D) Lines 48-52 ("All…home")

Prior question: The description of the incident (lines 58-66) primarily serves to

7. Which choice provides the best evidence…?

(A) Lines 61-63 ("For…parent")
(B) Lines 70-74 ("Behind…pressure")
(C) Lines 83-87 ("What…past")
(D) Lines 91-93 ("Much…goals")

Prior question: The diseases listed in line 8 mainly serve to

8. Which choice provides the best evidence…?

(A) Lines 10-14 ("As…causes")
(B) Lines 22-23 ("Much…origin")
(C) Lines 23-26 ("New…animals")
(D) Lines 30-32 ("Research…diseases")

Prior question: The question the narrator asks in lines 15-16 must nearly implies that

9. Which choice provides the best evidence…?

(A) Lines 1-4 ("Many…program")
(B) Lines 6-11 ("The fund…results")
(C) Lines 16-19 ("Through…news")
(D) Lines 23-24 ("But as…radio")

Prior question: The purpose of the fifth paragraph (lines 77-83) is to

10. Which choice provides the best evidence…?

(A) Lines 14-16 ("Every…ship")
(B) Lines 38-39 ("It is…cabins")
(C) Lines 57-59 ("The number…seasick")
(D) Lines 82-85 ("The range…activities")

Check the Answer Key on the next page.

ANSWER KEY

Reading Shortcut #2: Speed Practice Drill A

Line Number(s) in a Prior Question	Two Closest Answer Choices	Best Answer
1. line 21	1. A or B	1. A
2. line 19-22	2. C or D	2. C
3. lines 7-14	3. A or B	3. B
4. lines 65-72	4. C or D	4. C
5. lines 22-29	5. A or B	5. A
6. line 35	6. C or D	6. D
7. lines 58-66	7. A or B	7. B
8. line 8	8. A or B	8. A
9. lines 15-16	9. C or D	9. C
10. lines 77-83	10. C or D	10. D

SCORE BOX

Total Number of Correct Answers	Total Points Added to Your Score
1	10
2	20
3	30
4	40
5	50
6	60
7	70
8	80
9	90
10	100

Reminder: 1 correct answer adds roughly 10 points to your SAT score.

Shortcut #2:
Speed Practice Drill B

DIRECTIONS:
- ▶ Set your timer or timer app for 60 seconds.
- ▶ Underline the line number(s) stated in the prior question.
- ▶ Underline the 2 answer choices that are closest to the line numbers in the prior question.
- ▶ Circle 1 answer.

EXAMPLE
Prior Question: The central idea of lines <u>**69-80**</u> is to

Which 2 choices provide the best evidence…?
(A) Line 43 ("Media. . .life")
(B) Lines 49-56 ("Yet. . . motherland")
(C) <u>**Lines 65-75**</u> ("Society. . . home")
(D) <u>**Lines 81-82**</u> ("They. . . mediate")
Correct Answer: (C) or (D)

Experience the power you get to locate the 2 best answer choices in 2 seconds!

Prior question: The description of the parents in lines 16-24 primarily serves to
1. Which choice provides the best evidence…?
(A) Lines 4-6 ("An approach…dilemma")
(B) Lines 13-17 ("every…departure")
(C) Lines 35-40 ("Efforts…cope")
(D) Lines 41-45 ("Concern…parent")

Prior question: The question in paragraph 1 (lines 1-5) primarily serves to
2. Which choice provides the best evidence…?
(A) Lines 12-15 ("An…investigation")
(B) Lines 23-26 ("Adds…mystery")
(C) Lines 31-35 ("It is…art")
(D) Lines 47-50 ("What…value")

Prior question: The author's description (lines 35-39) suggests

3. **Which choice provides the best evidence…?**
(A) Lines 5-6 ("To prevent…network")
(B) Lines 36-38 ("But…global")
(C) Lines 43-46 ("Such a…forms")
(D) Lines 51-54 ("Now…done")

Prior question: The most likely purpose of the description in lines 5-6 is to

4. **Which choice provides the best evidence…?**
(A) Lines 17-23 ("Many…events")
(B) Lines 33-36 ("Perhaps…works")
(C) Lines 46-48 ("exposure…local")
(D) Lines 55-60 ("The question…use")

Prior question: The central idea of the third paragraph (lines 33-42) is that

5. **Which choice provides the best evidence…?**
(A) Lines 1-3 ("Much…photos")
(B) Lines 36-38 ("About…alone")
(C) Lines 49-54 ("To track…elders")
(D) Lines 61-64 ("The desire…family")

Prior question: In line 66, the word "select" most nearly means

6. **Which choice provides the best evidence…?**
(A) Lines 41-43 ("every…society")
(B) Lines 43-45 ("The person…himself")
(C) Lines 54-56 ("As…relations")
(D) Lines 67-72 ("The human…alone")

Prior question: The historical facts (lines 34-42) primarily support

7. **Which choice provides the best evidence?**
(A) Lines 1-4 ("To draw…historical")
(B) Lines 7-9 ("we…value")
(C) Lines 27-29 ("it…artist")
(D) Lines 33-36 ("Within…about")

Prior question: The supplies listed in lines 44-53 mainly serve to emphasize

8. **Which choice provides the best evidence?**
(A) Lines 54-57 ("Lonely…dog")
(B) Lines 58-60 ("The tent…strangers")
(C) Lines 66-68 ("Proud…first")
(D) Lines 72-75 ("Glad…supplies")

Prior question: The question the narrator asks in lines 14-15 most nearly implies that

9. **Which choice provides the best evidence…?**
(A) Lines 16-20 ("In this…time")
(B) Lines 26-28 ("How…free")
(C) Lines 53-54 ("The level…sports")
(D) Lines 57-61 ("Weekly…activities")

Prior question: The main purpose of the third paragraph (lines 28-33) is to

10. **Which choice provides the best evidence…?**
(A) Lines 41-44 ("Please…children")
(B) Lines 49-53 ("Issues…style")
(C) Lines 57-58 ("Remember…human")
(D) Lines 70-72 ("Many…school")

Check the Answer Key on the next page.

ANSWER KEY

Reading Shortcut #2: Speed Practice Drill B

Line Number(s) in a Prior Question	Two Closest Answer Choices	Best Answer
1. lines 16-24	1. B or C	1. B
2. lines 1-5	2. A or B	2. A
3. lines 35-39	3. B or C	3. B
4. lines 5-6	4. A or B	4. A
5. line 33-42	5. B or C	5. C
6. line 66	6. C or D	6. D
7. lines 34-42	7. C or D	7. D
8. lines 44-53	8. A or B	8. A
9. lines 14-15	9. A or B	9. B
10. lines 28-33	10. A or B	10. A

SCORE BOX

Total Number of Correct Answers	Total Points Added to Your Score
1	10
2	20
3	30
4	40
5	50
6	60
7	70
8	80
9	90
10	100

Reminder: 1 correct answer adds roughly 10 points to your SAT score.

DIRECTIONS:
- ▶ Set your timer or timer app for 60 seconds.
- ▶ Underline the line number(s) stated in the prior question.
- ▶ Underline the 2 answer choices that are closest to the line numbers in the prior question.
- ▶ Circle 1 answer.

EXAMPLE
Prior Question: The central idea of lines **69-80** is to

Which 2 choices provide the best evidence…?
(A) Line 43 ("Media. . .life")
(B) Lines 49-56 ("Yet. . . motherland")
(C) **Lines 65-75** ("Society. . . home")
(D) **Lines 81-82** ("They. . . mediate")
Correct Answer: (C) or (D)

Experience the power you get to locate the 2 best answer choices in 2 seconds!

Prior question: The description of the court (lines 34-39) primarily serves to
1. Which choice provides the best evidence…?
(A) Lines 48-52 ("Behind…court")
(B) Lines 60-63 ("The site…relation")
(C) Lines 70-73 ("Ask…among")
(D) Lines 81-83 ("What…copy")

Prior question: The author of Passage 1 identifies the people (Lines 11-15) as
2. Which choice provides the best evidence…?
(A) Lines 2-6 ("Yet…provide")
(B) Lines 10-19 ("To…them")
(C) Lines 34-35 ("The…evidence")
(D) Lines 81-82 ("In…testimony")

Prior question: The main idea of the third paragraph (lines 39-47) is to

3. Which choice provides the best evidence…?

(A) Lines 1-6 ("All…show")

(B) Lines 19-23 ("Much…start")

(C) Lines 41-46 ("But…dancing")

(D) Lines 52-57 ("We…live")

Prior question: The most likely purpose of the discussion in lines 14-19 is to

4. Which choice provides the best evidence…?

(A) Lines 5-6 ("At first…proposal")

(B) Lines 15-17 ("An…fund")

(C) Lines 21-24 ("A…discussion")

(D) Lines 33-38 ("With…statement")

Prior question: The central idea of the second paragraph (lines 35-49) is that

5. Which choice provides the best evidence…?

(A) Lines 5-8 ("every…women")

(B) Lines 19-20 ("To expect…an")

(C) Lines 33-42 ("By…gain")

(D) Lines 57-61 ("call…success")

Prior question: As used in line 5, the word "removed" most nearly means

6. Which choice provides the best evidence…?

(A) Lines 6-10 ("The team…day")

(B) Lines 11-18 ("Schools…sense")

(C) Lines 22-28 ("Parks…life")

(D) Lines 30-34 ("Larger…suburbs")

Prior question: The description of the countryside (lines 21-26) primarily serves to

7. Which choice provides the best evidence…?

(A) Lines 15-16 ("How…scenes")

(B) Lines 24-26 ("When…adults")

(C) Lines 27-30 ("the use…film")

(D) Lines 31-34 ("Constant…of")

Prior question: The types of model homes listed in lines 12-14 mainly emphasize

8. Which choice provides the best evidence…?

(A) Lines 4-8 ("the number…garages")

(B) Lines 13-18 ("All…family rooms")

(C) Lines 31-34 ("The typical…property")

(D) Lines 40-43 ("How…house")

Prior question: As used in line 12, the word "steel" most nearly means

9. Which choice provides the best evidence…?

(A) Lines 5-6 ("In…press")

(B) Lines 15-16 ("Their…rights")

(C) Lines 24-26 ("Ethical…changes")

(D) Lines 30-32 ("As…live")

Prior question: The purpose of the last lines (67-73) given to you in the passage is

10. Which choice provides the best evidence…?

(A) Lines 1-9 ("The attracts…fans")

(B) Lines 19-21 ("It…men")

(C) Lines 42-48 ("From…channel")

(D) Lines 63-69 ("It…sports")

Check the Answer Key on the next page.

ANSWER KEY

Reading Shortcut #2: Speed Practice Drill C

Line Number(s) in a Prior Question	Two Closest Answer Choices	Best Answer
1. lines 34-39	1. A or B	1. A
2. lines 11-15	2. B or C	2. B
3. lines 39-47	3. C or D	3. C
4. lines 14-19	4. B or C	4. B
5. lines 35-49	5. C or D	5. D
6. line 5	6. A or B	6. A
7. lines 21-26	7. B or C	7. B
8. lines 12-14	8. B or C	8. C
9. line 12	9. B or C	9. B
10. line 67-73	10. C or D	10. D

SCORE BOX

Total Number of Correct Answers	Total Points Added to Your Score
1	10
2	20
3	30
4	40
5	50
6	60
7	70
8	80
9	90
10	100

Reminder: 1 correct answer adds roughly 10 points to your SAT score.

Practice in Your SAT Workbooks

After completing the 3 Speed Practice Drills, you are the *all-seeing, all-knowing,* newly-minted **MASTER** of Reading Shortcut #2. Now you can put it to work for you.

Go to the Official SAT Study Guide published by The College Board which contains <u>real</u> SAT practice tests. Scan the reading section to see more examples of Shortcut #2. *Seeing is believing!* The more examples you see, the more this Shortcut will *stick* in your mind and give you the extra-scoring power you need to reach the score you want on your SAT test.

Nike tells you: *Just do it!*

Dr. Jay tells you: *Just use it!*

Just use it on every practice test you take, and you will be ready to snap up all the examples of Shortcut #2 hidden inside your SAT test.

No Shortcut is Foolproof

Just as there are exceptions to every rule, there are exceptions to **Reading Shortcut #2.**

READING SHORTCUT #3

RULE

<u>WHEN 1 answer choice to an SAT reading question contains a strong negative word(s),</u> such as *disdainful, hostile, or treacherous,* THEN this choice is a wrong answer.

SECRET PATTERN

1 answer choice contains a strong negative word:

(A)xxxxxxxxxxxxxxxxxxx
(B)xxxxxxxxxxxxxxxxxx
(C)xxxx **treacherous** xxx
(D)xxxxxxxxxxxxxxxxxxxx

REWARD

The second you RECOGNIZE this pattern you get the POWER to ELIMINATE 1 answer choice and PREDICT (A), (B), or (D) is the correct answer.

Reading Shortcut #3: EXAMPLES

The following 2 examples are SNAPSHOTS that show you how easy it is to recognize the **secret pattern** Shortcut #3 is based on: <u>**a strong negative word(s) in 1 answer choice.**</u>

EXAMPLE #1: BEFORE

Before you recognize the Shortcut, the SAT question is **difficult.** It is longer and harder to answer with 4 possible choices to read and think about.

1. The author's attitude toward the protestors can best be described as
   (A) hostile
   (B) disapproving
   (C) tolerant
   (D) sympathetic

❖   ❖   ❖   EXAMPLE #1: AFTER   ❖   ❖   ❖

After you recognize the Shortcut, the question is **simplified**. It is shorter and easier to answer with only 3 possible choices to read and think about.

1. The author's attitude toward the protestors can best be described as
   (B) disapproving
   (C) tolerant
   (D) sympathetic

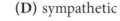

STRATEGY

Before you start to use the process of elimination (POE) to answer an SAT reading question, take **2 seconds** to scan the answer choices for this **secret pattern**: *a strong negative word(s) in 1 answer choice.*

DETECT

the strong negative word "hostile" in answer choice (A).

PREDICT

answer choice (A) is a wrong answer.
Rule out answer choice (A)!

DECIDE

either (B), (C), or (D) is the correct answer.
When you are totally clueless, just pick (B), (C), or (D).
By the law of chance, you **get a 33% chance** to select the correct answer.
When you have a clue to tip your decision in favor of (B), (C), or (D), go for it.
By using a bit of knowledge you **get a much higher than 33% chance** to select the correct answer.

SCORE

| 1 correct answer | *gives you* | 1 (raw) point |
| 1 (raw) point | *roughly adds* | 10 points to your SAT score! |

EXAMPLE #2: BEFORE

Before you recognize the Shortcut, the SAT question is **difficult**. It is longer and harder to answer with 4 possible choices to read and think about.

2. The author uses cooking and cleaning as examples (lines 15-18) primarily to
   (A) acknowledge that domestic tasks are time consuming
   (B) indicate that maintaining a home is a joint effort
   (C) convey that neglect of chores around the house can provoke resentment
   (D) point out the need for a division of labor

❖   ❖   ❖ EXAMPLE #2: AFTER ❖   ❖   ❖

After you recognize the Shortcut, the question is **simplified.** It is shorter and easier to answer with only 3 possible choices to read and think about.

2. The author uses cooking and cleaning as examples (lines 15-18) primarily to
   (A) acknowledge that domestic tasks are time consuming
   (B) indicate that maintaining a home is a joint effort
   (D) point out the need for a division of labor

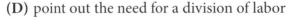

Before you start to use the process of elimination (POE) to answer an SAT reading question, take **2 seconds** to scan the answer choices for this **secret pattern**: *a strong negative word(s) in 1 answer choice.*

DETECT

the negative words "neglect" and "resentment" in answer choice (C).

PREDICT

answer choice (C) is a wrong answer.
Rule out answer choice (C)!

DECIDE

either (A), (B), or (D) is the correct answer.
When you are totally clueless, just pick (A), (B), or (D).
By the law of chance, you **get a 33% chance** to select the correct answer.
When you have a clue to tip your decision in favor or (A), (B), or (D), go for it.
By using a bit of knowledge you **get a much higher than 33% chance** to select the correct answer.

SCORE

| **1 correct answer** | *gives you* | **1 (raw) point** |
| **1 (raw) point** | *roughly adds* | **10 points to your SAT score!** |

The POWER of KNOWING How to Analyze Answer Choices

After seeing Reading Shortcut #3, you have the power of knowing exactly which secret pattern to look for in the answer choices that will give you an instant Shortcut to eliminate 1 answer choice you never recognized before.

Reading Shortcut #3: Speed Practice Drills

Now it is time to practice using Reading Shortcut #3 to access opportunities to score on your SAT in *a split-second – as fast as you click on Google or tap an app on your smartphone.* The questions in the drills are designed to develop your ability to rapidly scan the answer choices to detect this Shortcut: *a strong negative word(s) in 1 answer choice.*

The repetition built into the 3 drills will make scanning the answer choices for Reading Shortcut #3 a part of your test-taking routine – a new habit to locate the best answer choices faster than ever before possible. The faster you can recognize Shortcut #3 in the following drills the better prepared you will be to take advantage of this Shortcut to answer more questions and score more points on your SAT.

Reading Shortcut #3:
Speed Practice Drill A

DIRECTIONS:
- ▶ Set your timer or timer app for 60 seconds.
- ▶ Draw a line through the 1 answer choice in each question that contains a strong negative word(s).
- ▶ Circle 1 of the remaining answer choices – without thinking about the choices.

Experience the power you get to eliminate 1 answer choice in a split-second !

---

1. The passage indicates that the proposal was viewed with
- **(A)** reservations
- **(B)** disdain
- **(C)** ambivalence
- **(D)** optimism

2. The author characterizes the impact of the "social experiment" (lines 20-27) as
- **(A)** disturbing
- **(B)** hopeful
- **(C)** disastrous
- **(D)** predictable

3. The passage indicates that the narrator viewed "thinkers" (line 43) as
- **(A)** obnoxious
- **(B)** cautious
- **(C)** optimistic
- **(D)** flexible

4. The authors remarks in lines 56-64 are best described as
- **(A)** a forecast for a happy marriage
- **(B)** advice for a meaningful relationship
- **(C)** an acknowledgement of hostile feelings
- **(D)** insights to achieve mutual understanding

5. The imagery in Passage 1 is primarily intended to

(A) invoke a feeling of safety behind the wheel

(B) spark a desire to drive an SUV

(C) connect a new vehicle with the great outdoors

(D) convey potential danger on back roads

6. In the second paragraph (lines 30-43) the author's reference to pets primarily serves to

(A) point out that animal play is similar to child play

(B) suggest ways to teach children responsibility

(C) expand on the value of a home companion

(D) call attention to animal cruelty

7. The narrator refers to "Somalia" (lines 40-44) to make the point that

(A) immigrants are homesick in America

(B) jobs in hotels did not exist in Somalia

(C) life was intolerable in the villages

(D) families have to adjust to life in a city

8. The author of Passage 1 would most likely regard lines 57-62 in Passage 2 as evidence of the

(A) range of nonfiction books now in libraries

(B) popularity of violent graphic novels

(C) uneven quality of new books written for teens

(D) emergence of new categories of fiction

9. Paragraph two (lines 31-40) is best described as an

(A) expansion of the author's observations

(B) analysis of a disastrous flaw in the design of the study

(C) example of inflexible thinking

(D) exception to a widely held assumption

10. Passage 1 indicates that the counselor

(A) regarded helicopter parents as humorous

(B) found rude behavior infuriating

(C) considered success in college vital to success in life

(D) valued community service more than extracurricular activities

Check the Answer Key on the next page.

ANSWER KEY

Reading Shortcut #3: Speed Practice Drill A

Eliminate	Best Choices	Answer
1. B	1. A, C, or D	1. A
2. C	2. A, B, or D	2. B
3. A	3. B, C, or D	3. C
4. C	4. A, B, or D	4. B
5. D	5. A, B, or C	5. A
6. D	6. A, B, or C	6. B
7. C	7. A, B, or D	7. D
8. B	8. A, C, or D	8. A
9. B	9. A, C, or D	9. D
10. B	10. A, C, or D	10. C

SCORE BOX

Total Number of Correct Answers	Total Points Added to Your Score
1	10
2	20
3	30
4	40
5	50
6	60
7	70
8	80
9	90
10	100

Reminder: 1 correct answer adds roughly 10 points to your SAT score.

Reading Shortcut #3: Speed Practice Drill B

DIRECTIONS:
▶ Set your timer or timer app for 60 seconds.
▶ Draw a line through the 1 answer choice in each question that contains a strong negative word(s).
▶ Circle 1 of the remaining answer choices – without thinking about the choices.

Experience the power you get to eliminate 1 answer choice in a split-second!

1. The assumption made in lines 14-20 is primarily an indicator of
(A) forward-thinking
(B) narrow-mindedness
(C) ignorance
(D) optimism

2. In lines 31-40 the narrator's response to the dilemma shifts from
(A) fear to courage
(B) concern to worry
(C) doubt to certainty
(D) disapproval to support

3. In lines 24-29, the inclusion of the musician's remarks is primarily intended to
(A) call attention to an innovation
(B) demystify an outrageous image
(C) solicit a response for the audience
(D) highlight the thinking of a musical genius

4. In lines 2-21, the narrator's approach to resolving disputes can best be characterized as
(A) deliberate
(B) tactful
(C) intimidating
(D) judicious

5. The passage indicates that the narrator viewed the "fiscal crisis" (line 8) with
(A) disdain
(B) caution
(C) disbelief
(D) tolerance

6. The grandparents' comments in lines 65-69 primarily describes
(A) a sympathetic response to a unfortunate situation
(B) an acknowledgement of an intolerable circumstance
(C) an effort to avoid further family conflicts
(D) concern about the children's ability to cope

7. The author refers to "grassroots campaigns" (lines 12-23) in order to
(A) explain the impact of the movement on public opinion
(B) provide an example of effective door-to-door campaigning
(C) expose the negative effect of inflammatory advertising
(D) question the usefulness of last-minute phone calls

8. The author's reference to "a void" (lines 47-48) primarily suggests that
(A) every man is an island
(B) a person is responsible for his actions
(C) isolation is life-threatening
(D) humans are social animals

9. The primary purpose of the last paragraph is to
(A) suggest the ruthless nature of art collectors
(B) establish the value of art on the dark web
(C) expose the extensiveness of "fake art" forms
(D) draw a conclusion based on historical records

10. The passage indicates that the narrator views "sleep deprivation" (lines 35-47) as
(A) a cause of attention deficit disorder
(B) a vicious cycle that contributes to obesity
(C) an issue that requires lifestyle adjustments
(D) a reminder of the basic need for sleep

Check the Answer Key on the next page.

ANSWER KEY

Reading Shortcut #3: Speed Practice Drill B

Eliminate	Best Choices	Answer
1. C	1. A, B, or D	1. D
2. A	2. B, C, or D	2. B
3. B	3. A, C, or D	3. C
4. C	4. A, B, or D	4. A
5. A	5. B, C, or D	5. B
6. B	6. A, C, or D	6. C
7. C	7. A, B, or D	7. D
8. C	8. A, B, or D	8. B
9. A	9. B, C, or D	9. C
10. B	10. A, C, or D	10. A

SCORE BOX

Total Number of Correct Answers	Total Points Added to Your Score
1	10
2	20
3	30
4	40
5	50
6	60
7	70
8	80
9	90
10	100

Reminder: 1 correct answer adds roughly 10 points to your SAT score.

Reading Shortcut#3:
Speed Practice Drill C

DIRECTIONS:

▶ Set your timer or timer app for 60 seconds.

▶ Draw a line through the 1 answer choice in each question that contains a strong negative word.

▶ Circle 1 of the remaining answer choices – without thinking about the choices.

Experience the power you get to eliminate 1 answer choice in a split-second!

1. The second paragraph implies that the author felt

(A) out of place in a rural hospital
(B) concerned about the quality of care
(C) comfortable among other heart patients
(D) angry about needing surgery

2. The passage implies that the protestor's behavior was mainly caused by his

(A) disregard for authority
(B) deep frustration
(C) impatience with politics
(D) violent temper

3. In lines 43-55, the author of Passage 1 offers a perspective that is best defined as

(A) radical
(B) pacifist
(C) pragmatic
(D) sympathetic

4. In lines 41-53, the narrator indicates the community primarily views the nuclear power plant as

(A) threatening their health
(B) decreasing the value of their property
(C) increasing their job opportunities
(D) raising their anxiety about the future

5. The passage indicates that the narrator regards his physical trainer as a
(A) worthy opponent
(B) fearless drill sergeant
(C) zealous instructor
(D) cruel task master

6. The passage indicates that the narrator viewed romance(lines 12-24) as a
(A) natural part of a new courtship
(B) prerequisite for a good marriage
(C) burden to impose on a relationship
(D) unrealistic expectation

7. The narrator characterized a "blood sample"(lines 32-36) as necessary to
(A) provide clear and convincing evidence
(B) guard against condemning innocent people
(C) support the accuracy of eyewitness testimony
(D) ensure that justice is carried out

8. The passage suggests that the "silence" of the school board indicated
(A) animosity toward some members
(B) opposition to the proposal
(C) reluctance to continue the discussion
(D) impatience with the statement of half-truths

9. The author's description of "a girl in a newsroom"(lines 7-12) is primarily intended to
(A) expose extensive discrimination
(B) describe a struggle for credibility
(C) point out differences in policies
(D) provide evidence of favoritism

10. Both the authors of Passage 1 and Passage 2 regard the public as
(A) indifferent to political campaigns
(B) immune to reports of corporate scandal
(C) well-informed about their legal rights
(D) concerned about protecting their privacy

Check the Answer Key on the next page.

ANSWER KEY

Reading Shortcut #3: Speed Practice Drill C

Eliminate	Best Choices	Answer
1. D	1. A, B, or C	1. C
2. D	2. A, B, or C	2. B
3. A	3. B, C, or D	3. D
4. A	4. B, C, or D	4. B
5. D	5. A, B, or C	5. C
6. C	6. A, B, or D	6. A
7. B	7. A, C, or D	7. D
8. A	8. B, C, or D	8. C
9. A	9. B, C, or D	9. D
10. B	10. A, C, or D	10. A

SCORE BOX

Total Number of Correct Answers	Total Points Added to Your Score
1	10
2	20
3	30
4	40
5	50
6	60
7	70
8	80
9	90
10	100

Reminder: 1 correct answer adds roughly 10 points to your SAT score.

Practice in Your SAT Workbooks

After completing the 3 Speed Practice Drills, you are the *all-seeing, all-knowing,* newly-minted **MASTER** of Reading Shortcut #3. Now you can put it to work for you.

Go to the Official SAT Study Guide published by The College Board which contains <u>real</u> SAT practice tests. Scan the reading section to see more examples of Shortcut #3. *Seeing is believing!* The more examples you see, the more this Shortcut will *stick* in your mind and give you the extra-scoring power you need to reach the score you want on your SAT test.

> **Nike tells you:**   *Just do it!*
>
> **Dr. Jay tells you:** *Just use it!*
>
> *Just use it* on every practice test you take, and you will be ready to snap up all the examples of Shortcut #3 hidden inside your SAT test.

No Shortcut is Foolproof

Just as there are exceptions to every rule, there are exceptions to **Reading Shortcut #3.**

READING SHORTCUT #4

RULE

<u>**WHEN all the answer choices to an SAT reading question contain more than 1 line of text,** **THEN**</u> the longest answer choice is a wrong answer.

SECRET PATTERN

1 answer choice is longer than the other 3 choices:

(A) xxxxxxxxxxxxxxxxxxxxxxxxx
xxxxxxxxxxxxxxxxxxxxxx

(B) xxxxxxxxxxxxxxxxxxxxxxxxxx
xxxxxxxxxxxxxxxxxxx

(C) xxxxxxxxxxxxxxxxxxxxxxxx
xxxxxxxxxxxxxxxx

(D) xxxxxxxxxxxxxxxxxxxxxxxx
xxxxxxxxxxxxxxxxxxxxxxxxx
xxxxxxxxx

REWARD

The second you RECOGNIZE this pattern you get the POWER to ELIMINATE 1 answer choice and PREDICT (A), (B), or (C) is the correct answer.

Reading Shortcut #4: EXAMPLES

The following 2 examples are SNAPSHOTS that show you how easy it is to recognize the secret pattern Shortcut #4 is based on: **<u>1 answer choice is clearly longer than the other 3 choices.</u>**

EXAMPLE #1: BEFORE

Before you recognize the Shortcut, the SAT question is **difficult**. It is longer and harder to answer with 4 possible choices to read and think about.

1. What function does the fourth paragraph (lines 30-44) serve in the passage as a whole:
   - **(A)** It documents that a practice favored by the author has some merit and is worth further investigation.
   - **(B)** It supports with specific examples the argument presented in the previous paragraph.
   - **(C)** It introduces an alternative practice not addressed by the experts.
   - **(D)** It proposes abandoning a practice for which the passage provides some data.

❖   ❖   ❖ EXAMPLE #1: AFTER ❖   ❖   ❖

After you recognize the Shortcut, the question is **simplified**. It is shorter and easier to answer with only 3 possible choices to read and think about.

1. What function does the fourth paragraph (lines 30-44) serve in the passage as a whole:

   - **(B)** It supports with specific examples the argument presented in the previous paragraph.
   - **(C)** It introduces an alternative practice not addressed by the experts.
   - **(D)** It proposes abandoning a practice for which the passage provides some data.

Before you start to use the process of elimination (POE) to answer an SAT reading question, take 2 seconds to scan the answer choices for this **secret pattern:** *1 answer choice is clearly longer than the other 3 choices.*

DETECT

answer choice (A) is longer than the other 3 choices.

PREDICT

answer choice (A) is a wrong answer.
Rule out answer choice (A)!

DECIDE

either (B), (C), or (D) is the correct answer.

When you are totally clueless, just pick (B), (C), or (D).
By the law of chance, you **get a 33% chance** to select the correct answer.
When you have a clue to tip your decision in favor of (B), (C), or (D),
go for it.
By using a bit of knowledge you **get a much higher than 33% chance** to
select the correct answer.

SCORE

| 1 correct answer | *gives you* | 1 (raw) point |
| 1 (raw) point | *roughly adds* | 10 points to your SAT score! |

EXAMPLE #2: BEFORE

Before you recognize the Shortcut, the SAT question is **difficult.** It is longer and harder to answer with 4 possible choices to read and think about.

2. In lines 51-55, the author of Passage 2 refers to a statement made in Passage 1 in order to
   (A) raise a question about the qualifications of the author of Passage 1.
   (B) refute the position taken against female athletes in the first sentence of Passage 1.
   (C) call attention to the issues surrounding equal educational opportunity that are discussed by the author of Passage 2.

   (D) highlight points of agreement between the author of Passage 1 and the author of Passage 2.

❖ ❖ ❖ EXAMPLE #1: AFTER ❖ ❖ ❖

After you recognize the Shortcut, the question is **simplified**. It is shorter and easier to answer with only 3 possible choices to read and think about.

2. In lines 51-55, the author of Passage 2 refers to a statement made in Passage 1 in order to
   (A) raise a question about the qualifications of the author of Passage 1.
   (B) refute the position taken against female athletes in the first sentence of Passage 1.

   (D) highlight points of agreement between the author of Passage 1 and the author of Passage 2.

Before you start to use the process of elimination (POE) to answer an SAT reading question, take *2 seconds* to scan the answer choices for this **secret pattern:** *1 answer choice is clearly longer than the other 3 choices.*

DETECT

answer choice (C) is clearly longer than the other 3 choices.

PREDICT

answer choice (C) is a wrong answer.
Rule out answer choice (C)!

DECIDE

either (A), (B), or (D) is the correct answer.
When you are totally clueless, just pick (A), (B), or (D).
By the law of chance, you **get a 33% chance** to select the correct answer.
When you have a clue to tip your decision in favor of (A), (B), or (D), go for it.
By using a bit of knowledge you **get a much higher than 33% chance** to select the correct answer.

SCORE

| 1 correct answer | *gives you* | 1 (raw) point |
| 1 (raw) point | *roughly adds* | 10 points to your SAT score! |

The POWER of KNOWING How to Analyze Answer Choices

After seeing Reading Shortcut #4, you have the power of knowing exactly which secret pattern to look for in the answer choices that will give you an instant Shortcut to elimination 1 answer choice you never recognized before.

Reading Shortcut #4: Speed Practice Drill

Now it is time to practice using Reading Shortcut #4 to access opportunities to score on your SAT in *a split-second – as fast as you click on Google or tap an app on your smartphone.* The questions in the drill are designed to develop your ability to rapidly scan the answer choices to detect this Shortcut: *1 answer choice is clearly longer than the other 3 choices.*

The repetition built into the 3 drills will make scanning the answer choices for Reading Shortcut #4 a part of your test-taking routine — a new habit to locate the best answer choices faster than ever before possible. The faster you can snap up Shortcut #4 in the following drills, the better prepared you will be to take advantage of this Shortcut to answer more questions and score more points on your SAT.

Reading Shortcut #4: Speed Practice Drill A

DIRECTIONS:

▶ Set your timer or timer app for 30 seconds.

▶ Focus your attention on the length of the answer choices to each questions.

▶ Draw a line through the longest answer choice.

▶ Circle 1 of the remaining answer choices – without thinking about the choices.

Experience the power you get to eliminate 1 answer choice in a split-second!

1. In lines 19-26, the author of Passage 1 mentions several companies primarily to
(A) blablablablablablablablablabla blablabla
(B) blablablablablablablablabla blabla
(C) blablablablablablablabla blablablablabla
(D) blablablablablablablablablablabla blablablablablablablablablablabla

2. What function does the discussion of climate control serve in lines 25-34?
(A) blablablablablablablablablabla blablablablablablablablabla
(B) blablablablablablablablablabla blabla
(C) blablablablablablablabla blablablablabla
(D) blablablablablablablablablabla blablablabla

3. Based on the information in the passage, it can be reasonably inferred that

(A) blablablablablablablablablablablablabla blabla

(B) blablablablablablablablablablablabla blablablablablablablablablabla blablabla

(C) blablablablablablablablablabla blablablabla

(D) blablablablablablablablablablabla blablablablablablablablabla

4. Which statement best captures the author's central assumption in setting up his project?

(A) blablablablablablablabla blablablablabla

(B) blablablablablablablabla blablablabla

(C) blablablablablablablablablabla blablablablablablablablabla

(D) blablablablablablablablabla blabla

5. The passage identifies which of the following as a factor that contributed to the development of the super-highway

(A) blablablablablablablablablabla blablablablablablablablablabla blabla

(B) blablablablablablablablablablabla blablabla

(C) blablablablablablablabla blablablablablablablablabla

(D) blablablablablablablablablablabla blabla

6. According to the author of Passage 1, in order for the economy to progress, businessmen leaders must

(A) blablablablablablablablabla blablablablabla

(B) blablablablablablablablabla blablablablabla

(C) blablablablablablabla blablablablablablablablabla blablabla

(D) blablablablablablablabla blablabla

7. Which statement best describes the overall relationship between Passage 1 and Passage 2

(A) blablablablablablablablabla blablabla

(B) blablablablablablablabla blabla

(C) blablablablablablablabla blablabla

(D) blablablablablablablablabla blablablablablablablabla

8. In lines 45-52, the author of Passage 2 refers to a statement made in Passage 1 in order to

(A) blablablablablablablablabla blablablablabla

(B) blablablablablablablabla blablablablablablablablabla

(C) blablablablablabla blablablabla

(D) blablablablablablabla blablablablabla

9. The main purpose of the passage is to

(A) blablablablablablablablabla blabla

(B) blablablablablablablablabla blablabla

(C) blablablablablablablablabla blablablablablablablablabla

(D) blablablablablablablabla **bl**ablablablabla

10. Which statement is best supported by the data presented in the figure?

(A) blablablablablablablablabla blablablablablablablabla

(B) blablablablablablablabla blablablablablablablablabla

(C) blablablablablablablablabla blabla

(D) blablablablablablablablabla blablablablablablablabla blabla

Check the Answer Key on the next page.

ANSWER KEY

Reading Shortcut #4: Speed Practice Drill A

Eliminate	Best Choices	Answer
1. D	1. A, B, or C	1. A
2. A	2. B, C, or D	2. B
3. B	3. A, C, or D	3. C
4. C	4. A, B, or D	4. B
5. A	5. B, C, or D	5. D
6. C	6. A, B, or D	6. A
7. D	7. A, B, or C	7. C
8. B	8. A, C, or D	8. D
9. C	9. A, B, or D	9. B
10. D	10. A, B, or C	10. C

SCORE BOX

Total Number of Correct Answers	Total Points Added to Your Score
1	10
2	20
3	30
4	40
5	50
6	60
7	70
8	80
9	90
10	100

Reminder: 1 correct answer adds roughly 10 points to your SAT score.

Reading Shortcut #4:
Speed Practice Drill B

1. The main purpose of the opening statement of the passage is to
(A) blablablablablablablablablabla blablablblablablabla

(B) blablablablablablablablablabla blablablablablablablablablablabla

(C) blablablablablablablablablabla blablabla

(D) blablablablablablablablabla blablablablablablablablablabla blablabla

2. The author most likely uses examples in lines 9-17 of the passage to highlight the
(A) blablablablablablablablablabla blablabla

(B) blablablablablablablablablabla blablablabla

(C) blablablablablablablablablabla blablablablablablablablabla

(D) blablablablblablablablabla blablablabla

3. The central claim of Passage 1 is
(A) blablablablablablablablablablabla
blablablablablablablabla

(B) blablablablablablablablablabla
blablablablablablablablablablablabla

(C) blablablablablablablablabla
blablablablablabla

(D) blablablablablablablablabla
blablablablablabla

4. Which choice best describes what happens
in Passage 2?
(A) blablablablablablablablabla
blablablabla

(B) blablablablablablablabla
blablabla

(C) blablablablablablabla
blablablabla

(D) blablablablablablabla
blablablablablablablablabla

5. What function does the discussion of
Indian tribes serve in lines 50-58 in
Passage 1?
(A) blablablablablablablablablabla
blablablablablablablablablabla
blablabla

(B) blablablablablablablablabla
blablabla

(C) blablablablablablablabla
blablablablablablablabla

(D) blablablablablablablabla
blabla

6. What statement best describes the
relationship between the passages?
(A) blablablablablablablablabla
blabla

(B) blablablablablablabla
blablabla

(C) blablablablablablabla
blablablablabla

(D) blablablablablablabla
blablablablablablablablabla

7. The author's main purpose in including information on climate control in Passage 2 is to
(A) blablablablablablablablablabla blablablablablablabla
(B) blablablablablablablablabla blablablablablablabla
(C) blablablablablablablabla blablablablablablablablablabla
(D) blablablablablablablablabla blablabla

8. The graph following Passage 1 offers evidence that scientists
(A) blablablablablablablablablabla blablablablablablablablablablabla
(B) blablablablablablablablabla blablablabla
(C) blablablablablablablabla blablablablablabla
(D) blablablablablablablablabla blablablabla

9. The author of Passage 2 refers to The Old Man and the Sea primarily to suggest that
(A) blablablablablablablablablablabla blablablablabla
(B) blablablablablablablablablablabla blablablabla
(C) blablablablablablablablablabla blablablablabla
(D) blablablablablablablablablablabla blablablablablablablablablablabla

10. Which of the following points would the author of both passages most likely agree?
(A) blablablablablablablablablablabla blablabla
(B) blablablablablablablablablabla blablabla
(C) blablablablablablablablablabla blablablablablablablablablabla blablabla
(D) blablablablablablablablalbablabla blablabla

Check the Answer Key on the next page.

ANSWER KEY

Reading Shortcut #4: Speed Practice Drill B

Eliminate	Best Choices	Answer
1. D	1. A, B, or C	1. C
2. C	2. A, B, or D	2. B
3. B	3. A, C, or D	3. D
4. D	4. A, B, or C	4. A
5. A	5. B, C, or D	5. C
6. D	6. A, B, or C	6. A
7. C	7. A, B, or D	7. B
8. A	8. B, C, or D	8. D
9. D	9. A, B, or C	9. C
10. C	10. A, B, or D	10. D

SCORE BOX

Total Number of Correct Answers	Total Points Added to Your Score
1	10
2	20
3	30
4	40
5	50
6	60
7	70
8	80
9	90
10	100

Reminder: 1 correct answer adds roughly 10 points to your SAT score.

Reading Shortcut #4:
Speed Practice Drill C

1. The central problem the author describes in the passage is that
(A) blablablablablablablablabla blablablabla

(B) blablablablablablablablablabla blablablablblabla

(C) blablablablablablablablabla blablablabla

(D) blablablablablablablablablabla blablablablalblablablablabla

2. What statement is best supported by the data presented in the figure?
(A) blablablablablablablablablabla blablablablabla

(B) blablablablablablablablablabla blablablablablabla

(C) blablablablablablablablablabla blablablablabla

(D) blablablablablablablablablablabla blablablablablablablablabla

3. Based on the information in the passage, it can reasonably be inferred that
(A) blablablablablablablablablablablabla blablablablablablablablablablabla

(B) blablablablablablablablablablabla blablablablabla

(C) blablablablablablablablablablabla blablablablablablablablabla blablablabla

(D) blablablablablablablablablablabla blabla

4. The narrator implies that the author favors a type of distribution system that is
(A) blablablablablablablablablabla blabla

(B) blablablablablablablablablabla blablablablablablablablablablablabla

(C) blablablablablablablablablabla blablablabla

(D) blablablablablablablablablabla blablablablablabla

5. What function does the fourth paragraph (lines 40-54) serve in the passage as a whole?
(A) blablablablablablablablablablabla blablablablablablablablablabla blablablabla

(B) blablablablablablablablablabla blablablabla

(C) blablablablablablablablablabla blablablablablablablabla

(D) blablablablablablablablablabla blablablablablablablabla

6. What choice is supported by the data in the graph?
(A) blablablablablablablablablabla blablablablablabla

(B) blablablablablablablablabla blablalbablablabla

(C) blablablablablablablabla blablablablablablalbablabla blablabla

(D) blablablablablabblablablabla blablabla

7. What does the author suggest about the studies done in the 1990's?
(A) blablablablablablablablablablabla blablablablabla

(B) blablablablablablablablablablabla blabalblablabla

(C) blablablablablablablablablabla blablablablablablablablablabla

(D) blablablablablablablabla blablablabla

8. Which statement best captures the assumption made in lines 61- 72?
(A) blablablablablablablablabla blablablablablablablablabla blablabla

(B) blablablablablablablablabla blablablablablabla

(C) blablablablablablablablabla blablablablablablablabla

(D) blablablablalblablalblablabla blablablablablablablablabla

9. The author uses the example in the conclusion most likely to highlight
(A) blablablablablablablablablablabla blablablablablablablablablablabla

(B) blablablablablablablablablabla blablabla

(C) blablablablablablablablablabla blablablabla

(D) blablablablablablablablablablalba blablablablablabla

10. Which choice best summarizes the passage
(A) blablablablablablablablablabla blablablablabla

(B) blablablablablablablablablablabla blablablablablablablablablabla

(C) blablablablablablablabla blablablablabla

(D) blablablablablablablablabla blablabla

Check the Answer Key on the next page.

ANSWER KEY

Reading Shortcut #4: Speed Practice Drill C

Eliminate	Best Choices	Answer
1. D	1. A, B, or C	1. C
2. D	2. A, B, or C	2. B
3. C	3. A, B, or D	3. D
4. B	4. A, C, or D	4. A
5. A	5. B, C, or D	5. C
6. C	6. A, B, or D	6. B
7. C	7. A, B, or D	7. A
8. A	8. B, C, or D	8. D
9. A	9. B, C, or D	9. C
10. B	10. A, C, or D	10. A

SCORE BOX

Total Number of Correct Answers	Total Points Added to Your Score
1	10
2	20
3	30
4	40
5	50
6	60
7	70
8	80
9	90
10	100

Reminder: 1 correct answer adds roughly 10 points to your SAT score.

Practice in Your SAT Workbooks

After completing the practice drill, you are the ***all-seeing, all-knowing,*** newly minted **MASTER** of Reading Shortcut #4. Now you can put it to work for you.

Go to the Official SAT Study Guide published by The College Board which contains <u>real</u> SAT practice tests. Scan the reading section to see more examples of Shortcut #4. ***Seeing is believing!*** The more examples you see, the more this Shortcut will ***stick*** in your mind and give you the extra-scoring power you need to reach the score you want on your SAT test.

Nike tells you: ***Just do it!***

Dr. Jay tells you: ***Just use it!***

Just use it on every practice test you take, and you will be ready to snap up all the examples of Shortcut #4 hidden inside your SAT test.

No Shortcut is Foolproof

Just as there are exceptions to every rule, there are exceptions to **Reading Shortcut #4.**

WRITING SHORTCUT #5

**WHEN answer choices B, C, and D contain more than 1 word,
THEN the choice with the most words is a wrong answer.**

SECRET PATTERN
1 answer choice (B, C, or D) contains more words:

      (A) NO CHANGE
      (B) could have polluted river's
      (C) can pollute rivers,
      (D) has polluted river's

**The second you RECOGNIZE this pattern you get the POWER to
ELIMINATE 1 answer choice and PREDICT (A), (C) or (D) is the
correct answer.**

Writing Shortcut #5: EXAMPLES

The following 2 examples of Writing Shortcut #5 are SNAPSHOTS that show you how easy it is to recognize the **secret pattern** Shortcut #5 is based on: <u>**1 answer choice (B, C, or D) contains more words.**</u>

EXAMPLE #1: BEFORE

Before you recognize the Shortcut, the SAT question is **difficult.** It is longer and harder to answer with 4 possible choices to read and think about.

    (A) NO CHANGE
    (B) distant places.
    (C) distant of all places.
    (D) distant place in the world.

❖ ❖ ❖ EXAMPLE #1: AFTER ❖ ❖ ❖

After you recognize the Shortcut, the question is **simplified**. It is shorter and easier to answer with only 3 possible choices to read and think about.

    (A) NO CHANGE
    (B) distant places.
    (C) distant of all places.

Before you start to use the process of elimination (POE) to answer an SAT writing question, take *2 seconds* to scan the answer choices for this **secret pattern**: *1 answer choice (B, C, or D) contains more words.*

DETECT

answer choice (D) contains more words than (B) or (C).

PREDICT

answer choice (D) is a wrong answer.

DECIDE

either (A), (B) or (C) is the correct answer.
When you are totally clueless, just pick (A), (B) or (C).
By the law of chance, you **get a 33% chance** to select the correct answer.
When you have a clue to tip your decision in favor of (A), (B) or (C), go for it.
By using a bit of knowledge, you **get a much higher than 33% chance** to select the correct answer.

SCORE

| 1 correct answer | *gives you* | 1 (raw) point |
| 1 (raw) point | *roughly adds* | 10 points to your SAT score! |

EXAMPLE #2: BEFORE

Before you recognize the Shortcut, the SAT question is **difficult**. It is longer and harder to answer with 4 possible choices to read and think about.

(A) NO CHANGE
(B) initially begin their career
(C) start their career
(D) initiate a career

❖ ❖ ❖ EXAMPLE #2: AFTER ❖ ❖ ❖

After you recognize the Shortcut, the question is **simplified.** It is shorter and easier to answer with only 3 possible choices to read and think about.

(A) NO CHANGE
(C) start their career
(D) initiate a career

STRATEGY

Before you start to use the process of elimination (POE) to answer an SAT writing question, take *2 seconds* to scan the answer choices for this **secret pattern**: *1 answer choice (B, C, or D) contains more words.*

DETECT

answer choice (B) contains more words than (C) or (D).

PREDICT

answer choice (B) is a wrong answer.

DECIDE

either (A), (C), or (D) is the correct answer.
When you are totally clueless, just pick(A), (C) or (D).
By the law of chance, you **get a 33% chance** to select the correct answer
When you have a clue to tip your decision in favor of (A), (C) or (D), go for it.
By using a bit of knowledge, you **get a much higher than 33% chance** to select the correct answer.

SCORE

| 1 correct answer | *gives you* | 1 (raw) point |
| 1 (raw) point | *roughly adds* | 10 points to your SAT score! |

The POWER of KNOWING How to Analyze Answer Choices

After seeing Writing Shortcut #5, you have the power of knowing exactly which secret pattern to look for in the answer choices to writing questions that will give you an instant Shortcut to eliminate 1 answer choice you never recognized before.

Writing Shortcut #5: Speed Practice Drills

Now it is time to practice using Writing Shortcut #5 to access opportunities to score on your SAT in a ***split-second*** – *as fast as you click on Google or tap an app on your smartphone.* The questions in the drills are designed to develop your ability to rapidly scan the answer choices to detect this Shortcut to the correct answer: ***1 answer choice (B, C, or D) contains more words.***

The repetition built into the 3 drills will make scanning the answer choices for Writing Shortcut #5 a part of your test-taking routine – a new habit to locate the best answer choices faster than ever before possible. The faster you can snap up Shortcut #5 in the following drills, the better prepared you will be to take advantage of this Shortcut to answer more questions and score more points on your SAT.

Writing Shortcut #5:
Speed Practice Drill A

DIRECTIONS
▶ Set your timer or timer app for 60 seconds.
▶ Draw a line through the answer choice that contains the most words.
▶ Circle 1 of the remaining answer choices, without thinking about the choices.

Experience the power you get to eliminate 1 answer choice in a split-second!

1. (A) NO CHANGE
   (B) air travel, an idea
   (C) air travel. An idea
   (D) air travel, with the idea

2. (A) NO CHANGE
   (B) about the decline in jobs
   (C) about the job market
   (D) about fluctuations in the job market

3. (A) NO CHANGE
   (B) one week at a time
   (C) every so often
   (D) once in awhile

4. (A) NO CHANGE
   (B) it, builders
   (C) it, so the builders
   (D) it: builders

5. (A) NO CHANGE
   (B) increasing the zebra population
   (C) the zebra's multiplying
   (D) having more zebra's than other countries

6. (A) NO CHANGE
   (B) yard, and the
   (C) yard, and some people
   (D) yard, too, also the people

7. (A) NO CHANGE
   (B) analyzing, and the results can be
   (C) analyzing, as
   (D) analyzing when the results are

8. (A) NO CHANGE
   (B) but also contains a source of vitamin C
   (C) but also a source of vitamin C
   (D) and a source of vitamin C

9. (A) NO CHANGE
   (B) for their distribution
   (C) to be distributed by them
   (D) for distribution

10. (A) NO CHANGE
    (B) regulatory issues,
    (C) concerns related to regulations,
    (D) matters for the regulatory board of appeals

Check the Answer Key on the next page.

ANSWER KEY

Writing Shortcut #5: Speed Practice Drill A

Eliminate	Best Choices	Answer
1. D	1. A, B, or C	1. B
2. D	2. A, B, or C	2. A
3. B	3. A, C, or D	3. C
4. C	4. A, B, or D	4. D
5. D	5. A, B, or C	5. B
6. D	6. A, B, or C	6. C
7. B	7. A, C, or D	7. C
8. B	8. A, C, or D	8. D
9. B	9. A, C, or D	9. C
10. D	10. A, B, or C	10. B

SCORE BOX

Total Number of Correct Answers	Total Points Added to Your Score
1	10
2	20
3	30
4	40
5	50
6	60
7	70
8	80
9	90
10	100

Reminder: 1 correct answer adds roughly 10 points to your SAT score.

Writing Shortcut #5:
Speed Practice Drill B

DIRECTIONS
▶ Set your timer or timer app for 60 seconds
▶ Draw a line through the answer choice that contains the most words.
▶ Circle 1 of the remaining answer choices, without thinking about the choice.

Experience the power you get to eliminate 1 answer choice in a split-second!

1. (A) NO CHANGE
   (B) put in the journal of
   (C) published in
   (D) put into

2. (A) NO CHANGE
   (B) yearly, however,
   (C) per year,
   (D) each year, since

3. (A) NO CHANGE
   (B) job, graphic artist
   (C) job of graphic artist
   (D) job, know as graphic artist

4. (A) NO CHANGE
   (B) that are known to survive
   (C) which has survived
   (D) that have survived

5. (A) NO CHANGE
   (B) Consequently,
   (C) For this very reason,
   (D) Yet, this reason,

6. (A) NO CHANGE
   (B) dropped – by their team:
   (C) dropped by the team;
   (D) dropped by all the teams,

7. (A) NO CHANGE
   (B) or taken from them,
   (C) or taken from all of them,
   (D) or taken from, and

8. (A) NO CHANGE
   (B) scholars, and those who were
   (C) scholars – all of whom
   (D) scholars, who were

9. (A) NO CHANGE
   (B) all possibilities:
   (C) all possibilities, such as:
   (D) all possibilities –

10. (A) NO CHANGE
    (B) but also assisted
    (C) also assisted
    (D) but they also assisted

Check the Answer Key on the next page.

ANSWER KEY

Writing Shortcut #5: Speed Practice Drill B

Eliminate	Best Choices	Answer
1. B	1. A, C, or D	1. D
2. D	2. A, B, or C	2. B
3. D	3. A, B, or C	3. C
4. B	4. A, C, or D	4. A
5. C	5. A, B, or D	5. D
6. D	6. A, B, or C	6. C
7. C	7. A, B, or D	7. B
8. B	8. A, C, or D	8. A
9. C	9. A, B, or D	9. B
10. D	10. A, B, or C	10. B

SCORE BOX

Total Number of Correct Answers	Total Points Added to Your Score
1	10
2	20
3	30
4	40
5	50
6	60
7	70
8	80
9	90
10	100

Reminder: 1 correct answer adds roughly 10 points to your SAT score.

Writing Shortcut #5:
Speed Practice Drill C

DIRECTIONS
- ▶ Set your timer or timer app for 60 seconds
- ▶ Draw a line through the answer choice that contains the most words.
- ▶ Circle 1 of the remaining answer choices, without thinking about the choice.

Experience the power you get to eliminate 1 answer choice in a split-second!

1. (A) NO CHANGE
    (B) their responsibility
    (C) our responsibility
    (D) his or her responsibility

2. (A) NO CHANGE
    (B) tables, chairs and the couch
    (C) tables and chairs
    (D) tables, and other furniture

3. (A) NO CHANGE
    (B) however, they believe the problem
    (C) however; they believe that the problem,
    (D) however the problem,

4. (A) NO CHANGE
    (B) then, one by one
    (C) then, one by one,
    (D) then; one after the other

5. (A) NO CHANGE
    (B) My boss, Mr. Jones; who asked
    (C) My boss – Mr. Jones, asked
    (D) My boss, Mr. Jones, asked

6. (A) NO CHANGE
    (B) of no consequence, therefore,
    (C) of no consequence, nonetheless
    (D) of no consequence to them whatsoever,

7.   (A) NO CHANGE
    (B) supplied, but their
    (C) supplied, whereas
    (D) supplied by their peers

8.   (A) NO CHANGE
    (B) use devices for prediction
    (C) use specific devices to predict
    (D) use all available devices to make predictions

9.   (A) NO CHANGE
    (B) happy, and more
    (C) happier, than they were before
    (D) happier, and they were

10. (A) NO CHANGE
    (B) interested teachers and students
    (C) teachers and students who were interested
    (D) teacher's and student's interested

Check the Answer Key on the next page.

ANSWER KEY

Writing Shortcut #5: Speed Practice Drill C

Eliminate	Best Choices	Answer
1. D	1. A, B, or C	1. B
2. B	2. A, C, or D	2. D
3. C	3. A, B, or D	3. B
4. D	4. A, B, or C	4. C
5. B	5. A, C, or D	5. D
6. D	6. A, B, or C	6. B
7. D	7. A, B, or C	7. A
8. D	8. A, B, or C	8. C
9. C	9. A, B, or D	9. D
10. C	10. A, B, or D	10. B

SCORE BOX

Total Number of Correct Answers	Total Points Added to Your Score
1	10
2	20
3	30
4	40
5	50
6	60
7	70
8	80
9	90
10	100

Reminder: 1 correct answer adds roughly 10 points to your SAT score.

Practice in Your SAT Workbooks

After completing the 3 Speed Practice Drills, you are the ***all-seeing, all-knowing,*** newly-minted **MASTER** of Writing Shortcut #5. Now you can put it to work for you.

Go to the Official SAT Study Guide published by The College Board which contains <u>real</u> SAT practice tests. Scan the reading section to see more examples of Shortcut #5. ***Seeing is believing!*** The more examples you see, the more this Shortcut will ***stick*** in your mind and give you the extra-scoring power you need to reach the score you want on your SAT test.

Nike tells you: *Just do it!*

Dr. Jay tells you: *Just use it!*

Just use it on every practice test you take, and you will be ready to snap up all the examples of Shortcut #5 hidden inside your SAT test.

No Shortcut is Foolproof

Just as there are exceptions to every rule, there are exceptions to **Writing Shortcut #5.**

WRITING SHORTCUT #6

RULE

<u>WHEN 1 answer choice to an SAT writing questions contains
1 word that ends with "ing,"</u> THEN this choice is a wrong answer.

SECRET PATTERN

1 answer choice has a word that ends with "ing":

    (A) NO CHANGE
    (B) xxxxxxxxxxxx
    (C) protest**ing**
    (D) xxxxxxxxxxx

REWARD

The second you RECOGNIZE this pattern you get the POWER to
ELIMINATE 1 answer choice and PREDICT (A), (B), or (D) is the
correct answer.

WRITING SHORTCUT #6 EXAMPLES

The following 2 examples of Shortcut #6 are SNAPSHOTS that show you how easy it is to recognize the **secret pattern** Shortcut #6 is based on: **"ing" at the end of 1 word in 1 answer choice**.

EXAMPLE #1: BEFORE

Before you recognize the Shortcut, the SAT question is **difficult**. It is longer and harder to answer with 4 possible choices to read and think about.

1. **(A)** NO CHANGE
    (B) and suggesting
    (C) to suggest
    (D) suggests

❖ ❖ ❖ EXAMPLE #1: AFTER ❖ ❖ ❖

After you recognize the Shortcut, the SAT question is **simplified.** It is shorter and easier to answer with only 2 possible answer choices to read and think about.

1. **(A)** NO CHANGE
    (C) to suggest
    (D) suggests

STRATEGY

Before you start to use the process of elimination (POE) to answer an SAT writing question, take **2 seconds** to scan the answer choices for this secret pattern: **"ing" at the end of 1 word in 1 answer choice.**

DETECT

"ing" at the end of the word "suggesting" in answer choice (B).

PREDICT

(B) is the wrong answer.
Rule out answer choice (B)!

DECIDE

either (A), (C), or (D) is the correct answer.
When you are totally clueless, just pick (A), (C), or (D).
By the law of chance, you will **get a 33% chance** to select the correct answer.
When you have a clue to tip your decision in favor of (A), (C), or (D), go for it.
By using a bit of knowledge, you **get a much higher than 33%** chance to select the correct answer.

SCORE

| 1 correct answer | *gives you* | 1(raw) point |
| 1 (raw) point | *roughly adds* | 10 points to your SAT score! |

EXAMPLE #2: BEFORE

Before you recognize the Shortcut, the SAT question is **difficult**. It is longer and harder to answer with 4 possible choices to read and think about.

2. **(A)** NO CHANGE
   (B) to be distributed
   (C) for their distributing
   (D) for distribution

❖ ❖ ❖ EXAMPLE #2: AFTER ❖ ❖ ❖

After you recognize the Shortcut, the question is **simplified.** It is shorter and easier to answer with only 3 possible choices to read and think about.

2. **(A)** NO CHANGE
   (B) to be distributed
   (D) for distribution

Before you start to use the process of elimination (POE) to answer an SAT writing question, take **2 seconds** to scan the answer choices for this secret pattern: ***"ing" at the end of 1 word in 1 answer choice.***

DETECT

"ing" at the end of the word "distributing" in answer choice (C).

PREDICT

(C) is the wrong answer.
Rule out answer choice (C)!

DECIDE

either (A), (B), or (D).
When you are totally clueless, just pick (A), (B), or (D).
By the law of chance, you will **get a 33% chance** to select the correct answer.
When you have a clue to tip your decision in favor of (A), (B), or (D), go for it.
By using a bit of knowledge, you **get a much higher than 33% chance** to select the correct answer.

SCORE

| 1 correct answer | *gives you* | 1(raw) point |
| 1 (raw) point | *roughly adds* | 10 points to your SAT score! |

The POWER of KNOWING How to Analyze Answer Choices

After seeing Writing Shortcut #6, you have the power of knowing exactly which secret pattern to look for in the answer choices that will give you an instant Shortcut to eliminate 1 answer choice you never recognized before.

Writing Shortcut #6: Speed Practice Drills

Now it is time to practice using Shortcut #6 to access opportunities to score on your SAT in **2 seconds** – *as fast as you click on Google or tap an app on your smartphone*. The questions in the drills are designed to develop your ability to rapidly scan the answer choices to detect this Shortcut to the correct answer: ***"ing" at the end of 1 word in 1 answer choice.***

The repetition built into the 3 drills will make scanning the answer choices for Shortcut #6 a part of your test-taking routine – a new habit to locate the best answer choices faster than ever before possible. The faster you can snap up Shortcut #6 in the following drills, the better prepared you will be to take advantage of this Shortcut on your SAT test.

Writing Shortcut #6: Speed Practice Drill A

DIRECTIONS:

- ▶ Set your timer or timer app for 30 seconds.
- ▶ Draw a line through the 1 answer choice that has a word ending with "ing."
- ▶ Circle 1 of the remaining answer choices – without thinking about the choices.

Experience the power you get to eliminate 1 answer choice in a split-second!

1. **(A)** NO CHANGE
   (B) creating
   (C) produced
   (D) invented

2. **(A)** NO CHANGE
   (B) have questioned
   (C) questions
   (D) questioning

3. **(A)** NO CHANGE
   (B) officer stating
   (C) officer stated
   (D) officer's statement

4. **(A)** NO CHANGE
   (B) are striving
   (C) have strived
   (D) strive

5. **(A)** NO CHANGE
   (B) parent demanding
   (C) parent demanded
   (D) parent demand

6. **(A)** NO CHANGE
   (B) declines
   (C) to decline
   (D) and declining

7. **(A)** NO CHANGE
   (B) have earned
   (C) earns
   (D) earning

8. **(A)** NO CHANGE
   (B) also wanting
   (C) also wanted
   (D) but they also wanted

9. **(A)** NO CHANGE
   (B) they were
   (C) which were
   (D) those being

10. **(A)** NO CHANGE
    (B) reform
    (C) reforms
    (D) and reforming

Check the Answer Key on the next page.

ANSWER KEY

Writing Shortcut #6: Speed Practice Drill A

Eliminate	Best Choices	Answer
1. B	1. A, C, or D	1. A
2. D	2. A, B, or C	2. B
3. B	3. A, C, or D	3. C
4. B	4. A, C, or D	4. D
5. B	5. A, C, or D	5. C
6. D	6. A, B, or C	6. B
7. D	7. A, B, or C	7. A
8. B	8. A, C, or D	8. D
9. D	9. A, B, or C	9. C
10. D	10. A, B, or C	10. B

SCORE BOX

Total Number of Correct Answers	Total Points Added to Your Score
1	10
2	20
3	30
4	40
5	50
6	60
7	70
8	80
9	90
10	100

Reminder: 1 correct answer adds roughly 10 points to your SAT score.

Writing Shortcut #6:
Speed Practice Drill B

DIRECTIONS:

▶ Set your timer or timer app for 30 seconds.

▶ Draw a line through the 1 answer choice that has a word ending with "ing."

▶ Circle 1 of the remaining answer choice – without thinking about the choices.

Experience the power you get to eliminate 1 answer choice in a split-second!

1. **(A)** NO CHANGE
   (B) is being cleaned and pealed
   (C) are cleaned and peeled
   (D) came cleaned and peeled

2. **(A)** NO CHANGE
   (B) Keeping it as
   (C) It is kept as
   (D) Kept as

3. **(A)** NO CHANGE
   (B) the function of
   (C) functioning
   (D) have functioned

4. **(A)** NO CHANGE
   (B) are recalling
   (C) have recalled
   (D) recall

5. **(A)** NO CHANGE
   (B) to be restored by them
   (C) for their restoring
   (D) for restoration

6. **(A)** NO CHANGE
   (B) but also serving
   (C) but served
   (D) but they also serve

7. **(A)** NO CHANGE
   (B) instructs
   (C) to instruct
   (D) and instructing

8. **(A)** NO CHANGE
   (B) are
   (C) is now being
   (D) has been

9. **(A)** NO CHANGE
   (B) have survived
   (C) survives
   (D) surviving

10. **(A)** NO CHANGE
    (B) to be protected
    (C) for their protection
    (D) for protecting

Check the Answer Key on the next page.

ANSWER KEY
Writing Shortcut #6: Speed Practice Drill B

Eliminate	Best Choices	Answer
1. B	1. A, C, or D	1. C
2. B	2. A, C, or D	2. A
3. C	3. A, B, or D	3. D
4. B	4. A, C, or D	4. A
5. C	5. A, B, or D	5. B
6. B	6. A, C, or D	6. D
7. D	7. A, B, or C	7. C
8. C	8. A, B, or D	8. A
9. D	9. A, B, or C	9. C
10. D	10. A, B, or C	10. B

SCORE BOX

Total Number of Correct Answers	Total Points Added to Your Score
1	10
2	20
3	30
4	40
5	50
6	60
7	70
8	80
9	90
10	100

Reminder: 1 correct answer adds roughly 10 points to your SAT score.

Writing Shortcut #6:
Speed Practice Drill C

1. (A) NO CHANGE
   (B) and also demonstrates
   (C) but also demonstrates
   (D) demonstrating

2. (A) NO CHANGE
   (B) beginning their work
   (C) start their work
   (D) begin their work

3. (A) NO CHANGE
   (B) to draft
   (C) drafting
   (D) drafts

4. (A) NO CHANGE
   (B) will maintain
   (C) maintains
   (D) maintaining

5. (A) NO CHANGE
   (B) but also refusing
   (C) also refused
   (D) but they also refused

6. (A) NO CHANGE
   (B) whom uses
   (C) who using
   (D) who use

7. (A) NO CHANGE
   (B) being sorted and washed
   (C) are sorted and washed
   (D) to be sorted and washed

8. (A) NO CHANGE
   (B) have trained
   (C) trains
   (D) training

9. (A) NO CHANGE
   (B) by text messages
   (C) by texting
   (D) by text

10. (A) NO CHANGE
    (B) but also proposing
    (C) also proposed
    (D) but they also proposed

Check the Answer Key on the next page.

ANSWER KEY

Writing Shortcut #6: Speed Practice Drill C

Eliminate	Best Choices	Answer
1. D	1. A, B, or C	1. C
2. B	2. A, C, or D	2. A
3. C	3. A, B, or D	3. D
4. D	4. A, B, or C	4. A
5. B	5. A, C, or D	5. C
6. C	6. A, B, or D	6. D
7. B	7. A, C, or D	7. C
8. D	8. A, B, or C	8. B
9. C	9. A, B, or D	9. B
10. B	10. A, C, or D	10. A

SCORE BOX

Total Number of Correct Answers	Total Points Added to Your Score
1	10
2	20
3	30
4	40
5	50
6	60
7	70
8	80
9	90
10	100

Reminder: 1 correct answer adds roughly 10 points to your SAT score.

Practice in Your SAT Workbooks

After completing the 3 Speed Practice Drills, you are the ***all-seeing, all-knowing,*** newly-minted **MASTER** of Shortcut #6. Now you can put it to work for you.

Go to the Official SAT Study Guide published by The College Board which contains <u>real</u> SAT practice tests. Scan the reading section to see more examples of Shortcut #6. ***Seeing is believing!*** The more examples you see, the more this Shortcut will ***stick*** in your mind and give you the extra-scoring power you need to reach the score you want on your SAT test.

Nike tells you: *Just do it!*

Dr. Jay tells you: *Just use it!*

Just use it on every practice test you take, and you will be ready to snap up all the examples of Shortcut #6 hidden inside your SAT test.

No Shortcut is Foolproof

Just as there are exceptions to every rule, there are exceptions to **Writing Shortcut #6.**

MATH SHORTCUT #7

RULE

<u>WHEN all the answer choices to an SAT math question contain whole numbers</u>, THEN the lowest whole number is a wrong answer.

SECRET PATTERN
The lowest whole number is a wrong answer:

      (A)   **1**
      (B)   2
      (C)   4
      (D)   6

REWARD

The second you RECOGNIZE this pattern you get the POWER to ELIMINATE 1 answer choice and PREDICT (B), (C), or (D) is the correct answer.

Math Shortcut #7: EXAMPLES

The following 2 examples of Shortcut #7 are SNAPSHOTS that show you how easy it is to recognize the **secret pattern** Shortcut #7 is based on: <u>**the lowest whole number in the answer choices is a wrong answer.**</u>

EXAMPLE #1: BEFORE

Before you recognize the Shortcut, the question is **difficult.** It is longer and harder to answer with 4 possible answers to read and think about.

1. In figure x........, what is the value of y?
   (A)   2
   (B)   5
   (C)   7
   (D)   9

❖ ❖ ❖ EXAMPLE #1: AFTER ❖ ❖ ❖

After you recognize the Shortcut, the question is **simplified**. It is shorter and easier to answer with only 3 possible answers to read and think about.

1. In figure x........, what is the value of y?
   (B)   5
   (C)   7
   (D)   9

Before you start to use the process of elimination (POE) to answer an SAT math question, take *2 seconds* to scan the answer choices for this **secret pattern**: *the lowest whole number in the answer choices is a wrong answer.*

DETECT

the lowest whole number "2" in answer choice (A).

PREDICT

(A) is a wrong answer.
Rule out answer choice (A)!

DECIDE

either (B), (C), or (D) is the correct answer.
When you are totally clueless, just pick (B), (C), or (D).
By the law of chance, you **get a 33% chance** to select the correct answer.
When you plug in the numbers, you tip your decision in favor of (B), (C), or (D) and you **get a much higher than 33% chance** to select the correct answer.

SCORE

| 1 correct answer | *gives you* | 1 (raw) point |
| 1 (raw) point | *roughly adds* | 10 points to your SAT score! |

EXAMPLE #2: BEFORE

Before you recognize the Shortcut, the question is **difficult**. It is longer and harder to answer with 4 possible choices to read and think about.

2. In polygon *x*, how many triangles are formed?
   (A) 1
   (B) 0
   (C) 3
   (D) 5

❖ ❖ ❖ EXAMPLE #2: AFTER ❖ ❖ ❖

After you recognize the Shortcut, the question is **simplified**. It is shorter and easier to answer with only 3 possible choices to read and think about.

2. In polygon x, how many triangles are formed?
   (A) 1
   (C) 3
   (D) 5

Before you start to use the process of elimination (POE) to answer a math question, take *2 seconds* to scan the answer choices for this **secret pattern**: *the lowest whole number in the answer choices is a wrong answer.*

DETECT

the lowest whole number "0" in answer choice (B).

PREDICT

(B) is the wrong answer.
Rule out answer choice (B)!

DECIDE

either (A), (C), or (D) is the correct answer.
When you are clueless, just pick (A), (C), or (D).
By the law of chance, you **get a 33% chance** to select the correct answer.
When you plug in the numbers, you tip your decision in favor of (A), (C), or (D) and you **get a much higher than 33% chance** to select the correct answer.

SCORE

| 1 correct answer | *gives you* | 1 (raw) point |
| 1 (raw) point | *roughly adds* | 10 points to your SAT score! |

The POWER of KNOWING How to Analyze Answer Choices

After seeing Math Shortcut #7, you have the power of knowing exactly which secret pattern to look for in the answer choices that gives you an instant Shortcut to eliminate 1 answer choice you never recognized before.

Math Shortcut #7: Speed Practice Drills

Now it is time to practice using Math Shortcut #7 to access opportunities to score on your SAT in *2 seconds* – *as fast as you click on Google or tap an app on your Smartphone.* The questions in the following 3 drills are designed to develop your ability to rapidly scan the answer choices to detect this Shortcut to the correct answer: ***the lowest whole number is a wrong answer.***

The repetition built into the drills will make scanning the answer choices for Math Shortcut #7 a part of your test-taking routine – a new habit to locate the best answer faster than ever before possible. The faster you can snap up Shortcut #7 in the following drills, the better prepared you will be to take advantage of this Shortcut to answer more questions and score more points on your SAT.

Math Shortcut #7:
Speed Practice Drill A

DIRECTIONS:
- ▶ Set your timer or timer app for 30 seconds.
- ▶ Draw a line through the lowest whole number in the answer choices to each question.
- ▶ Circle 1 of the remaining 3 answer choices – without thinking about the choices.

Experience the power you get to eliminate 1 answer choice in a split-second!

1. In the figure above ....., what is the value of *x*?
   - (A) 2
   - (B) 4
   - (C) 5
   - (D) 8

2. For the numbers listed above....., what is the value of *n*?
   - (A) 3
   - (B) 4
   - (C) 8
   - (D) 1

3. For the positive integers....., which of the following is equal to *x-y*?
   - (A) 1
   - (B) 3
   - (C) 6
   - (D) 7

4. How many ordered pairs (x, y) can satisfy the equations above...?
   - (A) 0
   - (B) 1
   - (C) 2
   - (D) 3

5. If *x* and *y* are….., what is the value of *x*?
    (A) 1
    (B) 4
    (C) 2
    (D) 5

6. In the diagram above….., what is the value of the 3 pairs?
    (A) 46
    (B) 20
    (C) 32
    (D) 40

7. In the equation above….., what is the value of *z*?
    (A) 2
    (B) 4
    (C) 9
    (D) 10

8. In the polygon above….., how many triangles are formed?
    (A) five
    (B) four
    (C) three
    (D) two

9. In the operation described above….., what is the value of *x*?
    (A) 0
    (B) 1
    (C) 5
    (D) 7

10. When an integer is….., what number results?
    (A) 2
    (B) 3
    (C) 6
    (D) 9

Check the Answer Key on the next page.

ANSWER KEY

Math Shortcut #7: Speed Practice Drill A

Eliminate	Best Choices	Answer
1. A	1. B, C, or D	1. B
2. D	2. A, B, or C	2. C
3. A	3. B, C, or D	3. D
4. A	4. B, C, or D	4. B
5. A	5. B, C, or D	5. C
6. B	6. A, C, or D	6. A
7. A	7. B, C, or D	7. D
8. D	8. A, B, or C	8. A
9. A	9. B, C, or D	9. C
10. A	10. B, C, or D	10. B

SCORE BOX

Total Number of Correct Answers	Total Points Added to Your Score
1	10
2	20
3	30
4	40
5	50
6	60
7	70
8	80
9	90
10	100

Reminder: 1 correct answer adds roughly 10 points to your SAT score.

Math Shortcut #7:
Speed Practice Drill B

DIRECTIONS:
▶ Set your timer or timer app for 30 seconds.
▶ Draw a line through the lowest whole number in the answer choices to each question.
▶ Circle 1 of the remaining choices – without thinking about the choices.

Experience the power you get to eliminate 1 answer choice in a split- second!

1. In the figure above….., what is the value of *a*?
   (A) 0
   (B) 2
   (C) 5
   (D) 8

2. In the equation above….., what is the value of *m*, if…..?
   (A) 1
   (B) 0
   (C) 3
   (D) 5

3. Which of the following is the actual solution to the equation…..?
   (A) 1
   (B) 0
   (C) 3
   (D) 5

4. The angles shown are….., what is the value of *k*?
   (A) 2
   (B) 4
   (C) 6
   (D) 8

5. In the figure above….., which of the following is a possible value of *y*?
   (A) 0
   (B) 7
   (C) 8
   (D) 9

6. In the graph above….., what is the probability person *x* will be selected?
   (A) 3.0%
   (B) 6.0%
   (C) 8.0%
   (D) 9.0%

7. If a triangle….., what is the length of 1 side of the triangle?
   (A) 5
   (B) 4
   (C) 3
   (D) 2

8. In the figure above, what is the length of *CD*?
   (A) 10
   (B) 0
   (C) 2
   (D) 4

9. In the graph above….., what is the value of *z*?
   (A) 67
   (B) 73
   (C) 80
   (D) 92

10. In the equation above….., what is the value of *y*?
   (A) 5
   (B) 2
   (C) 6
   (D) 3

Check the Answer Key on the next page.

ANSWER KEY

Math Shortcut #7: Speed Practice Drill B

Eliminate	Best Choices	Answer
1. A	1. B, C, or D	1. B
2. B	2. A, C, or D	2. C
3. B	3. A, C, or D	3. D
4. A	4. B, C, or D	4. B
5. A	5. B, C, or D	5. D
6. A	6. B, C, or D	6. C
7. D	7. A, B, or C	7. A
8. B	8. A, C, or D	8. A
9. A	9. B, C, or D	9. B
10. B	10. A, C, or D	10. C

SCORE BOX

Total Number of Correct Answers	Total Points Added to Your Score
1	10
2	20
3	30
4	40
5	50
6	60
7	70
8	80
9	90
10	100

Reminder: 1 correct answer adds roughly 10 points to your SAT score.

DIRECTIONS:

▶ Set your timer or timer app for 30 seconds.

▶ Draw a line through the lowest whole number in the answer choices to each question.

▶ Circle 1 of the remaining answer choices –without thinking about the choices.

Experience the power you get to eliminate 1 answer choice in a split-second!

1. If a linear function….., what is the value of $x-y$?
   (A) 1
   (B) 2
   (C) 3
   (D) 6

2. In the figure above, what is the value of Z?
   (A) 0
   (B) 2
   (C) 4
   (D) 5

3. If m is a positive integer, then….. could equal which of the following?
   (A) 13
   (B) 9
   (C) 4
   (D) 2

4. In the above graph, what is the number of cases?
   (A) 4
   (B) 7
   (C) 11
   (D) 20

5. In a standard plane....., what is the length of *AB*?
   (A) 1
   (B) 4
   (C) 8
   (D) 12

6. In the graph above....., what is the value of *c*?
   (A) 3
   (B) 0
   (C) 5
   (D) 6

7. If fruit was added....., what is the weight of the basket?
   (A) two pounds
   (B) five pounds
   (C) seven pounds
   (D) eleven pounds

8. For the triangle above....., what is the length of *AB*?
   (A) 0
   (B) 6
   (C) 8
   (D) 12

9. If (y, z) is the solution to ....., what is the value of *z*?
   (A) 7
   (B) 5
   (C) 3
   (D) 1

10. In the graph provided above....., how much did the average household contribute to charity?
   (A) $9.00
   (B) $11.00
   (C) $20.00
   (D) $33.00

Check the Answer Key on the next page.

ANSWER KEY

Math Shortcut #7: Speed Practice Drill C

Eliminate	Best Choices	Answer
1. A	1. B, C, or D	1. C
2. A	2. B, C, or D	2. D
3. D	3. A, B, or C	3. B
4. A	4. B, C, or D	4. D
5. A	5. B, C, or D	5. B
6. B	6. A, C, or D	6. A
7. A	7. B, C, or D	7. C
8. A	8. B, C, or D	8. C
9. D	9. A, B, or C	9. A
10. A	10. B, C, or D	10. B

SCORE BOX

Total Number of Correct Answers	Total Points Added to Your Score
1	10
2	20
3	30
4	40
5	50
6	60
7	70
8	80
9	90
10	100

Reminder: 1 correct answer adds roughly 10 points to your SAT score.

Practice in Your SAT Workbooks

After completing the 3 practice drills, you are the ***all-seeing, all knowing***, newly-minted **MASTER** of Math Shortcut #7. Now you can put it to work for you.

Go to the Official SAT Study Guide published by The College Board which contains <u>real</u> SAT practice tests. Scan the reading section to see more examples of Shortcut #7. ***Seeing is believing!*** The more examples you see, the more this Shortcut will ***stick*** in your mind and give you the extra-scoring power you need to reach the score you want on your SAT test.

Nike tells you: *Just do it!*

Dr. Jay tells you: *Just use it!*

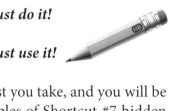

Just use it on every practice test you take, and you will be ready to snap up all the examples of Shortcut #7 hidden inside your SAT test.

No Shortcut is Foolproof

Just as there are exceptions to every rule, there are exceptions to **Math Shortcut #7.**

MATH SHORTCUT #8

RULE

<u>WHEN 2 answer choices to an SAT math question contain the same number(s) and/or letter(s)</u>, THEN 1 of these 2 choices is the correct answer.

SECRET PATTERN

2 answer choices contain the same number(s) and/or letter(s):

(A) xxxxxxxxxxxxx
(B) $x + b + (9 + 14)$
(C) $x + b + (9 + 3)$
(D) xxxxxxxxxxxxx

REWARD

The second you RECOGNIZE this secret pattern you get the POWER to ELIMINATE 2 answer choices and PREDICT (B) or (C) is the correct answer.

Math Shortcut #8: EXAMPLES

The following 2 examples of Shortcut #8 are SNAPSHOTS that show you how easy it is to recognize the **secret pattern** Shortcut #8 is based on: <u>**2 answer choices contain the same number(s) and/or letter(s). These 2 answer choices look the most alike.**</u>

EXAMPLE #1: BEFORE

Before you recognize the Shortcut, the SAT question is **difficult**. It is longer and harder to answer with 4 possible choices to read and think about.

1. In the figure above, what is the value of x?
   (A) $\sqrt{5}$
   (B) 8/3
   (C) 7
   (D) $2\sqrt{5}$

❖ ❖ ❖ EXAMPLE #1: AFTER ❖ ❖ ❖

After you recognize the Shortcut, the question is **simplified**. It is shorter and easier to answer with only 2 possible choices to read and think about.

1. In the figure above, what is the value of x?
   (A) $\sqrt{5}$
   (D) $2\sqrt{5}$

STRATEGY

Before you start to use the process of elimination (POE) to answer an SAT math question, take *2 seconds* to scan the answer choices for this **secret pattern**: *2 answer choices contain the same number(s) and/or letter(s). They look the most alike.*

DETECT

"$\sqrt{5}$" in answer choices (A) and (D).

PREDICT

(A) or (D) is the correct answer.
Rule out the other answer choices!

DECIDE

either (A) or (D).
When you are clueless, just pick (A) or (D).
By the law of chance, you **get a great 50% chance** to select the correct answer.
When you plug in the numbers, you tip your decision in favor of (A) or (D) and you **get a much higher than 50% chance** to select the correct answer.

SCORE

| 1 correct answer | *gives you* | 1(raw) point |
| 1 (raw) point | *roughly adds* | 10 points to your SAT score! |

EXAMPLE #2: BEFORE

Before you recognize the Shortcut, the SAT question is **difficult**. It is longer and harder to answer with 4 possible choices to read and think about.

1. In the table above….., what is the probability that the person belonged to Group A?
   (A) 5/120
   (B) 68/100
   (C) 79/130
   (D) 80/100

❖ ❖ ❖ EXAMPLE #2: AFTER ❖ ❖ ❖

After you recognize the Shortcut, the question is **simplified**. It is shorter and easier to answer with only 2 choices to read and think about.

1. In the table above….., what is the probability that the person belonged to Group A?
   (B) 68/100
   (D) 80/100

Before you start to use the process of elimination (POE) to answer an SAT question, take *2 seconds* to scan the answer choices for this **secret pattern**: *2 answer choices contain the same number(s) and/or letter(s). They look the most alike.*

DETECT

"*100*" in answer choices (B) and (D).

PREDICT

(B) or (D) is the correct answer.
Rule out the other answer choices!

DECIDE

either (B) or (D).
When you are clueless, just pick (B) or (D).
By the law of chance, you **get a great 50% chance** to select the correct answer.
When you plug in the numbers, you tip your decision in favor of (B) or (D) and you **get a much higher than 50% chance** to select the correct answer.

SCORE

1 correct answer	*gives you*	1 (raw) point
1 (raw) point	*roughly adds*	10 points to your SAT score!

The POWER of KNOWING How to Analyze Answer Choices

After seeing Shortcut #8, you have the power of knowing exactly which **secret pattern** to look for in the answer choices that will give you an instant Shortcut to identify the 2 best answer choices you never recognized before.

Math Shortcut #8: Speed Practice Drills

Now it is time to practice using Shortcut #8 to access opportunities to score on your SAT in a *split-second* – *as fast as you click on Google or tap an app on your Smartphone.* The questions in the drills are designed to develop your ability to rapidly scan the answer choices and detect this Shortcut to the answer: *2 answer choices contain the same number(s) and/or letter(s). They look the most alike.*

The repetition built into the 3 drills will make scanning the answer choices for Math Shortcut #8 a part of your test-taking routine – a new habit to locate the best answer choices faster than ever before possible. The faster you can snap up Shortcut #8 in the following drills, the better prepared you will be to take advantage of this Shortcut to answer more questions and score more points on your SAT test.

DIRECTIONS:
▶ Set your timer or timer app for 60 seconds.
▶ Underline the 2 answer choices that are "the most alike" in each question.
▶ Circle 1 answer choice – without thinking about either choice.

Experience the power you get to identify the 2 best answer choices in a split-second!

1. In the map above….., how many miles are the boys from the park?
   (A) 40
   (B) 51.5
   (C) 56.5
   (D) 75

2. In the figure above….., what is the distance from vertex *F* to vertex *G*?
   (A) $3\sqrt{2}$
   (B) $3\sqrt{3}$
   (C) 4
   (D) 6

3. In the figure above….., what is the value of *y*?
   (A) 108
   (B) 114
   (C) 117
   (D) 120

4. According to the chart above….., what fraction of guests attended the dinner?
   (A) 13/42
   (B) 5/16
   (C) 8/20
   (D) 17/42

5. If….., which of the following represents the total change?
   (A) 150 + 20c
   (B) 160 + 10
   (C) 160 + 10z
   (D) 170 + 30c

6. In the figure above….., what is the perimeter of *ABCD*?
   (A) 2
   (B) 4
   (C) $8\sqrt{2}$
   (D) $10\sqrt{2}$

7. In the figure above, at what time was the tank full?
   (A) 1:18
   (B) 2:25
   (C) 4:00
   (D) 4:30

8. In the recipe above….., how many cups of flour were required?
   (A) 6 1/2
   (B) 8
   (C) 10 1/3
   (D) 10 2/3

9. According to the chart above….., how many minutes will it take to fill the tank?
   (A) 4.1
   (B) 2.5
   (C) 3.4
   (D) 4.7

10. In the graph above….., what is the weight of the package in pounds?
    (A) 2 1/3
    (B) 4
    (C) 1 1/3
    (D) 6 3/4

Check the Answer Key on the next page.

ANSWER KEY
Math Shortcut #8: Speed Practice Drill A

Best Choices	Answer
1. B or C	1. B
2. A or B	2. B
3. B or C	3. C
4. A or D	4. A
5. B or C	5. C
6. C or D	6. D
7. C or D	7. C
8. C or D	8. D
9. A or D	9. A
10. A or C	10. C

SCORE BOX

Total Number of Correct Answers	Total Points Added to Your Score
1	10
2	20
3	30
4	40
5	50
6	60
7	70
8	80
9	90
10	100

Reminder: 1 correct answer adds roughly 10 points to your SAT score.

Math Shortcut #8:
Speed Practice Drill B

DIRECTIONS:
- ▶ Set your timer or timer app for 30 seconds.
- ▶ Underline the 2 answer choices that are "the most alike" in each question.
- ▶ Circle 1 answer choice – without thinking about either choice.

Experience the power you get to identify the 2 best answer choices in a split-second!

---

1. In the figure above….., what is the length of the cord?
   (A)   10 feet
   (B)   15 feet
   (C) $20\sqrt{2}$ feet
   (D) $20\sqrt{3}$ feet

2. In the xy-plane above….., what is the value of p?
   (A)   2 1/2
   (B)   4 3/5
   (C)   6 3/4
   (D)   10 1/2

3. In the figure above….., what is the value of y/x?
   (A)   2/5
   (B)   3/4
   (C)   3/5
   (D)   1/3

4. If x is increased by 20% and y is decreased by 20%….., what is the ratio of x to y?
   (A)   2/3
   (B)   3/5
   (C)   1/1
   (D)   4/5

5. What is the solution to the system of equations above
   (A) -3,-1
   (B) -5, 2
   (C) 3, -1
   (D) 2, 1

6. The square cube above has….., what is the length of diagonal AB?
   (A) 4
   (B) $5\sqrt{2}$
   (C) $5\sqrt{3}$
   (D) 6

7. If….., what is the average of p, r, and s?
   (A) p + r
   (B) p + x/5
   (C) p + 2x/5
   (D) p + 2r/2

8. In the rectangle above….., what is the value of y?
   (A) 7
   (B) 4/5
   (C) 3
   (D) 2/5

9. In the diagram above….., what is the probability…..?
   (A) 5/10
   (B) 8/10
   (C) 9/12
   (D) 11/15

10. In the equation above….., what is the value of 5x + 3y?
    (A) -5
    (B) 5/8
    (C) -6
    (D) 7/8

Check the Answer Key on the next page.

ANSWER KEY

Math Shortcut #8: Speed Practice Drill B

Best Choices	Answers
1. C or D	1. C
2. A or D	2. A
3. A or C	3. C
4. B or D	4. D
5. A or C	5. C
6. B or C	6. B
7. B or C	7. B
8. B or D	8. D
9. A or B	9. A
10. B or D	10. B

SCORE BOX

Total Number of Correct Answers	Total Points Added to Your Score
1	10
2	20
3	30
4	40
5	50
6	60
7	70
8	80
9	90
10	100

Reminder: 1 correct answer adds roughly 10 points to your SAT score.

Math Shortcut #8:
Speed Practice Drill C

1. In the sequence above….., how much greater is term x than term Z?
   (A) 152
   (B) 157
   (C) 182
   (D) 190

2. In the scatter gram….., how many data points would be above the line $z = y$?
   (A)   2
   (B)   5
   (C) -2
   (D)   8

3. If $y + 2 =$….., what is the value of y?
   (A) 0.75
   (B) 1.22
   (C) 2.75
   (D) 3.00

4. If x time is spent….., how many minutes are spent online each day?
   (A)   70
   (B) 242
   (C) 342
   (D) 360

5. If x, y, and z are….., what is the greatest value of z?
   (A) 3.4
   (B) 2.0
   (C) 4.5
   (D) 4.7

6. If integer k is….., what is the value of m?
   (A) -4
   (B) -2
   (C) 0
   (D) 2

7. In the figure above….., what is the value of $a + b + c + d$?
   (A) 268
   (B) 137
   (C) 264
   (D) 46

8. If set X consists of….., what is the probability….?
   (A) 19/40
   (B) 29/100
   (C) 9/50
   (D) 21/50

9. In the equation above….., what is the relationship between x and y?
   (A) $x = 1y - 2$
   (B) $x = 1 (y - 10)$
   (C) $x = 10 - 2y$
   (D) $x = 10 - y$

10. John saved his paycheck until he had ….. After 1 year, what is the value of y?
    (A) $9,708
    (B) $5,400
    (C) $4,350
    (D) $1,400

Check the Answer Key on the next page.

ANSWER KEY

Math Shortcut #8: Speed Practice Drill C

Best Choices	Answer
1. A or B	1. B
2. A or C	2. A
3. A or C	3. C
4. B or C	4. C
5. C or D	5. D
6. B or D	6. B
7. A or C	7. C
8. C or D	8. D
9. C or D	9. D
10. B or D	10. B

SCORE BOX

Total Number of Correct Answers	Total Points Added to Your Score
1	10
2	20
3	30
4	40
5	50
6	60
7	70
8	80
9	90
10	100

Reminder: 1 correct answer adds roughly 10 points to your SAT score.

Practice in Your SAT Workbooks

After completing the 3 practice drills, you are the *all-seeing, all-knowing*, newly-minted **MASTER** of Math Shortcut #8. Now you can put it to work for you.

Go to the Official SAT Study Guide published by The College Board which contains <u>real</u> SAT practice tests. Scan the reading section to see more examples of Shortcut #8. *Seeing is believing!* The more examples you see, the more this Shortcut will *stick* in your mind and give you the extra-scoring power you need to reach the score you want on your SAT test.

Nike tells you:	*Just do it!*	
Dr. Jay tells you:	*Just use it!*	

Just use it on every practice test you take, and you will be ready to snap up all the examples of Shortcut #8 hidden inside your SAT test.

No Shortcut is Foolproof

Just as there are exceptions to every rule, there are exceptions to **Math Shortcut #8.**

BONUS SHORTCUT:
Find Mistakes Fast

In addition to using Shortcuts to find answers faster than ever before possible, you can also use Shortcuts to find your mistakes faster. This Bonus Shortcut reveals a pattern in the SAT Answer Key for the Math, No-Calculator Section which has a total of 15 questions.

is

The SAT distributes the correct answers across all the letter choices: A, B, C, and D. In the Math, No-Calculator Section each letter choice is the correct answer to a minimum of 3 questions.
WHEN each letter choice (A, B, C, and D) is NOT recorded as your answer to 3 questions in the Math, No-Calculator Section, THEN you can find mistakes fast.

SECRET PATTERN

Letter choice (A) is the correct answer to a minimum of 3 questions
Letter choice (B) is the correct answer to a minimum of 3 questions
Letter choice (C) is the correct answer to a minimum of 3 questions
Letter choice (D) is the correct answer to a minimum of 3 questions.

Student Letter Choice Tally:
The number of times each letter choice is recorded as your answer:

$$
\begin{array}{rcl}
(A) & = & 2 \\
(B) & = & 6 \\
(C) & = & 4 \\
(D) & = & 3 \\
\end{array}
$$

Total = 15
Letter Choice Used Less than 3 Times: (A)
Minimum Number of Mistakes: 1

The second you RECOGNIZE you only selected letter choice (A) as your answer to 2 questions, you get the POWER to FIND 1 MISTAKE FAST. You can correct this 1 mistake by changing 1 answer to letter choice (A).

Bonus Shortcut: EXAMPLES

The following 2 examples give you a SNAPSHOT that shows you how easy it is to recognize the **secret pattern** this Bonus Shortcut is based on: <u>**each letter choice (A, B, C, and D) is the correct answer to a minimum of 3 questions in the Math, No-Calculator Section.**</u>

EXAMPLE #1: FIND MISTAKES FAST

Math, No Calculator Section

Student Answer Sheet

1. (A) (B) (C) (D)
2. (A) (B) (C) (D)
3. (A) (B) (C) (D)
4. (A) (B) (C) (D)
5. (A) (B) (C) (D)
6. (A) (B) (C) (D)
7. (A) (B) (C) (D)
8. (A) (B) (C) (D)
9. (A) (B) (C) (D)
10. (A) (B) (C) (D)
11. (A) (B) (C) (D)
12. (A) (B) (C) (D)
13. (A) (B) (C) (D)
14. (A) (B) (C) (D)
15. (A) (B) (C) (D)

Student Letter Choice Tally:

(A) = 4
(B) = 5
(C) = 1
(D) = 5

Total = 15

Letter Choice Used Less than 3 Times: (C)

Minimum Number of Mistakes to Correct: 2

Before you check your answers in chronological order (question 1, question 2, question 3, etc.), tally the number of times you used each letter choice (A, B, C, and D) in the No-Calculator Math Section to identify this **secret pattern**: *any letter choice not recorded as your answer to 3 questions.*

DETECT

letter choice (C) is recorded as your answer to only 1 question.

PREDICT

letter choice (C) is the correct answer to 2 additional questions.

CHECK

the questions in which letter choice (C) was your <u>second choice</u>. Change 2 answers to letter choice (C).

SCORE

| 1 correct answer | *gives you* | 1 (raw) point |
| 1 (raw) point | *roughly adds* | 10 points to your SAT score! |

EXAMPLE #2: FIND MISTAKES FAST

Math, No Calculator Section

Student Answer Sheet

1. Ⓐ Ⓑ Ⓒ Ⓓ
2. Ⓐ Ⓑ Ⓒ Ⓓ
3. Ⓐ Ⓑ Ⓒ Ⓓ
4. Ⓐ Ⓑ Ⓒ Ⓓ
5. Ⓐ Ⓑ Ⓒ Ⓓ
6. Ⓐ Ⓑ Ⓒ Ⓓ
7. Ⓐ Ⓑ Ⓒ Ⓓ
8. Ⓐ Ⓑ Ⓒ Ⓓ
9. Ⓐ Ⓑ Ⓒ Ⓓ
10. Ⓐ Ⓑ Ⓒ Ⓓ
11. Ⓐ Ⓑ Ⓒ Ⓓ
12. Ⓐ Ⓑ Ⓒ Ⓓ
13. Ⓐ Ⓑ Ⓒ Ⓓ
14. Ⓐ Ⓑ Ⓒ Ⓓ
15. Ⓐ Ⓑ Ⓒ Ⓓ

Student Letter Choice Tally:

(A) = 5
(B) = 2
(C) = 4
(D) = 4

Total = 15

Letter Choice Used Less than 3 Times: (B)

Minimum Number of Mistakes to Correct: 1

Before you check your answers in chronological order (question 1, question 2, question 3, etc.) tally the number of times you used each letter choice (A, B, C, and D) in the No-Calculator Math Section to identify this secret pattern: *any letter choice not recorded as your answer to 3 questions.*

DETECT

letter choice (B) is recorded as your answer to only 2 questions.

PREDICT

letter choice (B) is the correct answer to 1 additional question.

CHECK

the questions in which letter choice (B) was your <u>second choice</u>. Change 1 answer to letter choice (B).

SCORE

| 1 correct answer | *gives you* | 1 (raw) point |
| 1 (raw) point | *roughly adds* | 10 points to your SAT score! |

The POWER of KNOWING How to Analyze Answer Choices

After seeing the Bonus Shortcut, you have the power of knowing exactly which secret pattern to look for in your student answer sheet that will give you a Shortcut to find your mistakes faster than ever before possible.

Bonus Shortcut: Speed Practice Drills

Now it is time to practice using this Bonus Shortcut to find mistakes in your answer sheet in a **split-second** – as *fast as you click on Google or tap an app on your Smartphone*. The drills are designed to develop your ability to rapidly scan your answer sheet to detect this Shortcut in the Math, No-Calculator Section: ***each letter choice is the correct answer to a minimum of 3 questions.***

The repetition built into the 3 drills will make scanning the answer choices for this Bonus Shortcut a part of your test-taking routine — a new habit to locate your mistakes fast. The faster you can find your mistakes in the following drills, the better prepared you will be to take advantage of this Bonus Shortcut to reach your highest possible SAT score.

Bonus Shortcut:
Speed Practice Drill A

DIRECTIONS:
▶ Set your timer or timer app for 30 seconds.
▶ Count the number of times you used each letter choice in your answers.
▶ Record the letter choice you used less than 3 times.
▶ Record the number of mistakes to correct.

MATH: NO CALCULATOR SECTION

Student Answer Sheet

1. Ⓐ **Ⓑ** Ⓒ Ⓓ
2. Ⓐ Ⓑ Ⓒ **Ⓓ**
3. Ⓐ Ⓑ **Ⓒ** Ⓓ
4. Ⓐ **Ⓑ** Ⓒ Ⓓ
5. Ⓐ Ⓑ **Ⓒ** Ⓓ
6. Ⓐ **Ⓑ** Ⓒ Ⓓ
7. Ⓐ Ⓑ Ⓒ **Ⓓ**
8. Ⓐ Ⓑ **Ⓒ** Ⓓ
9. Ⓐ **Ⓑ** Ⓒ Ⓓ
10. **Ⓐ** Ⓑ Ⓒ Ⓓ
11. Ⓐ **Ⓑ** Ⓒ Ⓓ
12. Ⓐ Ⓑ Ⓒ **Ⓓ**
13. Ⓐ Ⓑ **Ⓒ** Ⓓ
14. Ⓐ Ⓑ Ⓒ **Ⓓ**
15. **Ⓐ** Ⓑ Ⓒ Ⓓ

Student Letter Choice Tally:

A = _____
B = _____
C = _____
D = _____

Total = _____

Letter Choice Used Less than 3 Times: _____

Minimum Number of Mistakes to Correct: _____

Check the Answer Key on page 150.

Bonus Shortcut:
Speed Practice Drill B

DIRECTIONS:

▶ Set your timer or timer app for 30 seconds.
▶ Count the number of times you used each letter choice.
▶ Record the letter choice you used less than 3 times.
▶ Record the number of mistakes to correct.

MATH: NO-CALCULATOR SECTION

Student Answer Sheet

1. (A) (B) (C) **(D)**
2. (A) (B) **(C)** (D)
3. (A) **(B)** (C) (D)
4. (A) (B) **(C)** (D)
5. (A) (B) (C) **(D)**
6. (A) (B) **(C)** (D)
7. (A) (B) (C) **(D)**
8. (A) **(B)** (C) (D)
9. (A) **(B)** (C) (D)
10. (A) **(B)** (C) (D)
11. (A) (B) **(C)** (D)
12. (A) **(B)** (C) (D)
13. (A) (B) (C) **(D)**
14. **(A)** (B) (C) (D)
15. (A) (B) **(C)** (D)

Student Letter Choice Tally:

A = _____
B = _____
C = _____
D = _____

Total = _____

Letter Choice Used Less than 3 Times: _____

Minimum Number of Mistakes to Correct: _____

Check the Answer Key on page 150.

Bonus Shortcut:
Speed Practice Drill C

DIRECTIONS:
- ▶ Set your timer or timer app for 30 seconds.
- ▶ Count the number of times you used each letter choice in your answers.
- ▶ Record the letter choice you used less than 3 times.
- ▶ Record the number of mistakes to correct.

MATH: NO-CALCULATOR SECTION

Student Answer Sheet

1. Ⓐ Ⓑ **Ⓒ** Ⓓ
2. **Ⓐ** Ⓑ Ⓒ Ⓓ
3. Ⓐ Ⓑ Ⓒ **Ⓓ**
4. Ⓐ Ⓑ Ⓒ **Ⓓ**
5. Ⓐ Ⓑ Ⓒ **Ⓓ**
6. Ⓐ **Ⓑ** Ⓒ Ⓓ
7. Ⓐ Ⓑ Ⓒ **Ⓓ**
8. **Ⓐ** Ⓑ Ⓒ Ⓓ
9. **Ⓐ** Ⓑ Ⓒ Ⓓ
10. Ⓐ Ⓑ **Ⓒ** Ⓓ
11. Ⓐ Ⓑ Ⓒ **Ⓓ**
12. Ⓐ **Ⓑ** Ⓒ Ⓓ
13. Ⓐ Ⓑ Ⓒ **Ⓓ**
14. Ⓐ **Ⓑ** Ⓒ Ⓓ
15. **Ⓐ** Ⓑ Ⓒ Ⓓ

Student Letter Choice Tally:

A = _____
B = _____
C = _____
D = _____

Total = _____

Letter Choice Used Less than 3 Times: _____

Minimum Number of Mistakes to Correct: _____

Check the Answer Key on page 150.

ANSWER KEY

Bonus Math Shortcut: Speed Practice Drill A
Student Letter Choice Tally

A = 2
B = 5
C = 4
D = 4

Letter Choice Used Less than 3 Times: A
Minimum Number of Mistakes to Correct: 1

Plan to check the questions in which A was your <u>second choice</u>.
Change 1 answer to letter choice A.

ANSWER KEY

Bonus Shortcut: Speed Practice Drill B
Student Letter Choice Tally

A = 1
B = 4
C = 6
D = 4

Letter Choice Used Less than 3 Times: A
Minimum Number of Mistakes to Correct: 2

Plan to check the questions in which (A) was your <u>second choice</u>.
Change 2 answers to letter choice (A).

ANSWER KEY

Bonus Shortcut: Speed Practice Drill C
Student Letter Choice Tally

A = 3
B = 3
C = 2
D = 7

Letter Choice Used Less than 3 Times: C
Minimum Number of Mistakes to Correct: 1

Plan to check the questions in which C was your <u>second choice</u>.
Change 1 answer to letter choice C.

Practice in Your SAT Workbooks

After completing the 3 practice examples, you are the **all-seeing, all-knowing**, newly-minted **MASTER** of this Bonus Shortcut that shows you how to find a mistake fast.

Go to the Official SAT Study Guide published by The College Board which contains <u>real</u> SAT practice tests. Scan the reading section to see more examples of this Bonus Shortcut. **Seeing is believing!** The more examples you see, the more this Shortcut will **stick** in your mind and give you the extra-scoring power you need to reach the score you want on your SAT test.

Nike tells you: *Just do it!*

Dr. Jay tells you: *Just use it!*

Just use it on every practice test you take, and you will be ready to snap up all the examples of this Bonus Shortcut hidden inside your SAT test.

No Shortcut is Foolproof

Just as there are exceptions to every rule, there are exceptions to this **Bonus Shortcut.**

PART III
TOP 3 SAT VOCABULARY SECRETS

SHORTCUTS

Top 3 SAT Vocabulary Secrets

There is only so much time you can devote to developing your SAT vocabulary. Here are 3 vocabulary secrets that will immediately save you time and simplify your approach to learning SAT vocabulary words. *The more vocabulary secrets you know, the less you will stress over the vocabulary you will see in your SAT.*

SAT Vocabulary Secret #1: All the SAT Words You Need to Know Are in the Answer Choices

 STOP thinking the SAT is a vocabulary test and you should learn the meaning of every odd word you come across in print, online, or hear anywhere.

 START focusing on learning the meaning of the words you come across in the answer choices to SAT questions.

If you have taken a few practice tests, you have already seen some of the popular words that often appear in the answer choices, such as ambiguous, cynical, and equitable. Make it your top priority to learn the meaning of ALL the words in the answer choices you cannot define. *The more words in the answer choices you can define, the easier it is to answer SAT questions.*

SAT Vocabulary Secret #2: All You Really Need to Know is a 1-Word Definition

 STOP thinking you need to develop in-depth knowledge of the meaning of words to be prepared to answer all the challenging questions in the reading section of the SAT.

 START thinking you only need to develop a basic knowledge of the meaning of words to be prepared to answer all the challenging questions in the reading section of the SAT.

The basic knowledge you need is a 1-word definition or synonym. For example, you need to know that the word "ambiguous" means unclear but you do not need to expand on this knowledge and also memorize that "ambiguous" means vague, hard to understand, and open to more than one interpretation. The 1-word definition "unclear" is just enough information about what "ambiguous" means for you to be able to either: 1) eliminate this word in the answer choices to a SAT question or 2) consider this word a possible answer to a question.

SAT Vocabulary Secret #3: You Can Instantly Memorize the Basic Meaning of SAT Words by Using First-Letter-Links

 STOP slowly memorizing words by reading and writing the words over and over again.

 START instantly memorizing words by using First-Letter-Links.

First-Letter-Links is a mnemonic strategy that enormously speeds up the process of memorizing the basic meaning of SAT vocabulary words by matching the first 3 letters (or more) at the beginning of an **unfamiliar word** with the first three letters (or more) at the beginning of a **familiar word** in your vocabulary. The use of the same 3 letters at the beginning of both the unfamiliar and familiar word creates a strong visual clue that sticks in your mind like glue and makes it possible for you to memorize the basic meaning of a word in a matter of seconds.

First-Letter-Links Memorization Strategy

Challenge yourself to use First-Letter-Links to memorize the basic meaning of words in the following list. Select 4 unfamiliar words. You can memorize the basic meaning of 1 word in less than 30 seconds and 4 words in less than 2 minutes. This means: You can use First-Letter-Links to memorize 100 SAT words in 50 minutes. You can also use First-Letter-Links to memorize vocabulary or key terms in all the challenging courses you are taking in high school. **First-Letter-Links gives you a fast memorization strategy to prepare for the SAT and to prepare for all the multiple-choice tests you take in high school and in college.**

	SAT Word	Triple-Letter-Link	Basic Meaning
1.	**acc**rue (v.)	link **acc** with **accumulate**	**accumulate**
2.	**allev**iate (v.)	link **allev** with **Aleve**	**relieve**
3.	**antiq**uated (adj.)	link **antiq** with **antique**	**old**
4.	**app**licable (adj.)	link **app** with **applied**	**able to be applied**
5.	**ard**uous (adj.)	link **ard** with **hard**	**difficult**
6.	**arti**san (n.)	link **arti** with **artist**	**artist**
7.	as**simil**ation (n.)	link **simil** with **similar**	**make similar**
8.	**aud**ible (adj.)	link **aud** with audio	**able to be heard**
9.	**ban**ish (v.)	link **ban** with **banned books**	**thrown out**

10.	**bene**volent (adj.)	link **bene** with **beneficial**	**benefitting others**
11.	**bla**nd (adj.)	link **bla** with **tastes bla**	**mild**
12.	**boo**rish (adj.)	link **boo** with **booing**	**rude**
13.	**brea**ch (n.)	link **brea** with **break**	**break a law**
14.	**bre**vity (adj.)	link **bre** with **brief**	**brief**
15.	**bro**ach (v.)	link **br** with **bring up**	**bring up a subject**
16.	**cap**ricious (adj.)	link **cap** with **changing caps**	**changeable**
17.	**car**icature (n.)	link **car** with **cartoon**	**cartoon sketch**
18.	**chi**de (v.)	link **chi** with **scold a child**	**scold**
19.	**circu**itous (adj.)	link **circu** with circular	**round about**
20.	**copi**ous (adj.)	link **copi** with many **copies**	**plentiful**
21.	**cover**t (adj.)	link **cover** with **cover up**	**conceal**
22.	**cred**ible (adj.)	link **cred** with **creed and beliefs**	**believable**

23.	**dorm**ant (adj.)	link **dorm** with **sleep**	**inactive**
24.	**dub**ious (adj.)	link **dub** with **doubt**	**doubtful**
25.	**dup**licity (n.)	link **dup** with **duped**	**deceive**
26.	**dur**able (adj.)	link **dur** with **enduring**	**lasting**
27.	**duti**ful (adj.)	link **duti** with **duty**	**obedient**
28.	**ed**ify (v.)	link **ed** with **educate**	**educate**
29.	**eff**icacious (adj.)	link **eff** with **effective**	**effective**
30.	**ego**centric (adj.)	link **ego** with **self**	**self-centered**
31.	**ener**vate (v.)	link **ener** with **drain energy**	**drain strength**
32.	**erro**neous (adj.)	link **erro** with **error**	**wrong**
33.	**equ**itable (adj.)	link **equ** with **equal**	**fair**
34.	**escal**ation (n.)	link **escal** with **escalator**	**rising intensity**
35.	**exempl**ary (adj.)	link **exempl** with **example**	**good example**

36.	estraneous (adj.)	link **estra** with **excessive**	**excessive**
37.	façade (n.)	link **fac** with **face**	**outward appearance**
38.	fallacy (n.)	link **fal** with **false**	**not true**
39.	flaccid (adj.)	link **fla** with **flabby**	**flabby**
40.	fortuitous (adj.)	link **fortu** with **fortune**	**by chance**
41.	frenetic (adj.)	link **fren** with **frenzied**	**frenzied**
42.	garrulous (adj.)	link **gar** with **Gary is talkative**	**talkative**
43.	genteel (adj.)	link **gent** with **gentleman**	**polished**
44.	glacial (adj.)	link **glac** with **glacier**	**ice**
45.	grievous (adj.)	link **grie** with **grief**	**causing grief**
46.	imminent (adj.)	link **imm** with **immediate**	**about to happen**
47.	impetuous (adj.)	link **imp** with **impulsive**	**impulsive**
48.	judicious (adj.)	link **jud** with **judge**	**sound judgement**

49.	laborious (adj.)	link **labor** with **work**	hard work
50.	lackluster (adj.)	link **lack** with **lack brightness**	dull
51.	longevity (n.)	link **long** with **long life**	long life
52.	magnanimous (adj.)	link **mag** with **magnificently generous**	generous
53.	mediocre (adj.)	link **medi** with **medium**	medium quality
54.	mystic (adj.)	link **myst** with **mysterious**	mysterious
55.	negligible (adj.)	link **neg** with **negative**	little value
56.	ominous (adj.)	link **omin** with **bad omen**	foreshadowing evil
57.	pallid (adj.)	link **pal** with **pale**	pale
58.	perilous (adj.)	link **peril** with **danger**	dangerous
59.	pertinent (adj.)	link **pert** with **pertains to**	relevant
60.	plethora (n.)	link **ple** with **plentiful**	excessive
61.	pragmatic (adj.)	link **pra** with **practical**	practical

62.	**preten**tious (adj.)	link **preten** with **pretend**	**pretend to be important**
63.	**propr**iety (n.)	link **propr** with **proper**	**proper behavior**
64.	**pun**ative (adj.)	link **pun** with **punish**	**inflict punishment**
65.	**pur**ge (v.)	link **pur** with **purify**	**cleanse**
66.	**que**ry (n.)	link **que** with **question**	**question**
67.	**quie**scent (adj.)	link **quie** with **quiet**	**quiet**
68.	**repl**enish (v.)	link **repl** with **replace**	**replace**
69.	**res**pite (n.)	link **res** with **rest**	**temporary rest**
70.	**rever**e (v.)	link **rever** with **reverence**	**regard with reverence**
71.	**sacr**osanct (adj.)	link **sacr** with **sacred**	**hold sacred**
72.	**sag**acious (adj.)	link **sag** with **sage**	**wise**
73.	**sati**ate (adj.)	link **sati** with **satisfied**	**completely full**
74.	**serpent**ine (adj.)	link **serpent** with **snake**	**snakelike**

75.	servile (adj.)	link serv with servant who is	submissive
76.	slovenly (adj.)	link slo with sloppy	sloppy
77.	solidarity (n.)	link solid with solid support	unity
78.	sonorous (adj.)	link son with sound	producing sound
79.	spatial (adj.)	link spa with space	occur in space
80.	stratagem (n.)	link strat with strategy	strategy to deceive
81.	stringent (adj.)	link stri with strict	strict
82.	stupor (n.)	link stu with stun	stunned condition
83.	suffice (v.)	link suffi with sufficient	sufficient
84.	sullen (adj.)	link sul with sulk	sulky
85.	supercilious (adj.)	link super with superior	act superior
86.	terrestrial (adj.)	link terr with terrain	related to Earth
87.	timorous (adj.)	link tim with timid	timid

88.	**total**itarian (adj.)	link **total** with **total control**	**total control**
89.	**tre**pidation (n.)	link **tre** with **tremble**	**trembling**
90.	**val**orous (adj.)	link **val** with **valiant**	**valiant**
91.	**vacu**ous (adj.)	link **vacu** with **vacuum**	**empty**
92.	**varie**gated (adj.)	link **varie** with **varied**	**varied appearance**
93.	**verb**ose (adj.)	link **verb** with **words**	**wordy**
94.	**vigil**ant (adj.)	link **vigil** with **keep a vigil**	**watchful**
95.	**vil**ify (v.)	link **vil** with **villain**	**make evil statements**
96.	**vir**ulent (adj.)	link **vir** with **virus**	**highly infectious**
97.	**voc**iferous (adj.)	link **voc** with **vocal**	**shouting voice**
98.	**vol**atile (adj.)	link **vol** with **volcano**	**explosive**
99.	**volum**inous (adj.)	link **volum** with **volume**	**great volume**
100.	**wis**tful (adj.)	link **wis** with **wishful**	**wishful, longing for**

PART IV
YOUR POWER-SCORING GEAR

SHORTCUTS

At the Top of Your Game

You used the combination of Shortcuts and the process of elimination (POE) on your SAT practice tests and definitely found **2 strategies were better than 1!** When a practice test question contained a Shortcut, you snapped it up in *2 seconds* to identify the best answer choices fast. For all the practice test questions that did not contain a Shortcut, you relied on the more deliberate process of elimination (POE) to determine the answer.

By adding Shortcuts to your SAT game plan you reached your SAT goal on your practice test. Your score went up 50 to 200 points! You are now "at the top of your game" and ready to take advantage of all the opportunities you know the Shortcuts will give you to achieve the same results on your real SAT as you achieved on your practice test.

The Scoring Advantage of Each Shortcut is In Your Hands

Reading Shortcut #1: When 2 answer choices to an SAT reading question contain the same word(s), you now have the power to identify the 2 best answers in a split-second.

· ·

Reading Shortcut #2: When an SAT reading question asks for the "best evidence," you now have the power to identify the 1 best answer in a split-second.

· ·

Reading Shortcut #3: When 1 answer choice to an SAT reading question contains a strong negative word, you now have the power to eliminate this answer choice in a split-second.

· ·

Reading Shortcut #4: When all the answer choices to an SAT reading question contain more than 1 line of text, you now have the power to eliminate the longest answer choice in a split-second.

· ·

Writing Shortcut #5: When 1 answer choice to an SAT writing question contains more words, you now have the power to eliminate this answer choice in a split-second.

· ·

Writing Shortcut #6: When 1 answer choice to an SAT writing question contains 1 word that ends with "ing," you now have the power to eliminate this answer choice in a split-second.

Math Shortcut #7: When all the answer choices to an SAT math question contain whole numbers, you now have the power to eliminate the lowest whole number in the answer choices in a split-second.

Math Shortcut #8: When 2 answer choices to an SAT math question contain the same number(s) and/or letter(s), you now have the power to identify the 2 best answer choices in a split-second.

Bonus Shortcut: When each letter choice (A, B, C, and D) is not recorded as your answer to 3 questions in the Math No-Calculator Section, you now have the power to find mistakes in your answer sheet in a split-second.

The Vocabulary Secrets are At Your Fingertips

SAT Vocabulary Secret #1: Focus on Answer Choice Words
The most important SAT words you need to know are the words that appear in the answer choices to SAT questions.

SAT Vocabulary Secret #2: Learn Just the Most Basic Definition
The most basic, 1 word definition of a word is all you really need to know to be able to either eliminate an answer choice or consider an answer choice as a possible answer to a question.

SAT Vocabulary Secret #3: First-Letter-Links Give You a Fast Memorization Strategy
The first 3 letters at the beginning of a SAT vocabulary word give you a strong visual clue to help you memorize the basic meaning of a word in 30 seconds or less.

FAST FORWARD to Your SAT Test Day
As I always say to my students:

May the Shortcuts be with you!

Walk IN to Your SAT
Ready to snap up Shortcuts to:

Maximize your score fast!

Walk OUT of Your SAT
Knowing you took advantage of many Shortcuts to:

Reach your SAT goal and
Open the doors of more colleges to you!

INDEX

About the Author

Over the course of her career, Dr. Jay has taught at the elementary, middle, high school, and post-secondary level; and analyzed student performance on standardized, multiple-choice tests at each of these levels. This extensive experience contributes to Dr. Jay's expertise in decoding the patterns hidden inside SAT questions and converting the patterns to SAT Shortcuts. Dr. Jay's research and consulting work at the National Institute for Research on Teaching, the National Institute of Education, the National Education Goals Panel, the Connecticut State Department of Education, and the Commonwealth of Massachusetts Department of Education expand her expertise in educational assessment and her background to create the first pattern-recognition strategy for the SAT. Hundreds of students have thanked Dr. Jay for teaching them how to identify patterns in SAT questions that give them instant Shortcuts to the answers.

Follow Dr. Jay on Facebook, Twitter, and Instagram for daily tips and SAT shortcuts @ **DrJayShortcuts**.